30 DAY

PASSAGEWAY TO

REVIVAL

PRAYER CALENDAR & JOURNAL

David C Woodrum

DESTINY IMAGE® PUBLISHERS, INC.
P.O. Box 310, Shippensburg, PA 17257-0310
"Promoting Inspired Lives."

This book and all other Destiny Image and Destiny Image Fiction books are available at Christian bookstores and distributors worldwide.

For more information on foreign distributors, call
717-532-3040.
Or reach us on the Internet: www.destinyimage.com

ISBN 13 TP: 978-0-7684-4335-6
ISBN 13 eBook: 978-0-7684-4336-3

For Worldwide Distribution, Printed in the U.S.A.

1 2 3 4 5 6 7 8 9 10 11 /22 21 20 19 18 17

INDEX of CONTENTS

4   Dedication

5   Introduction

6   30 Day Calendar of Prayer

67   List of Targeted Focus Items for Prayer

WHY FAST... When the Lord has provided so bountifully?

74   The Importance of Fasting

77   Some of the Values of Fasting

82   Various Lengths of Fasting

85   Loss of Benefits – The Motive for Fasting

86   How to Fast

88   Practical Tips for Fasting

91   Other Forms of Fasting

92   A Few Fasting Scriptures

94   List of **'One Another'** Scriptures

100 Postscript

101 Other titles available from David C. Woodrum

<u>DEDICATION</u>

I would like to respectfully acknowledge the influence of Nate Krupp in my life. Several of his writings are included within the content of the HOJSPM Associate Degree Bible College curriculum which is presently being utilized among more than sixty (60) locations in thirteen (13) countries. One of those books; **"THE CHURCH TRIUMPHANT AT THE END OF THE AGE"** greatly affected my life in so many ways that I cannot adequately express my appreciation.

Additionally, his example of prayer and commitment to mobilizing 'Concerted Prayer for Revival' since I first met him in 1988 has been a source of encouragement.

I dedicate this book to your legacy. Thank you.

30 Day Passageway to Revival

As you join with others in this **30-Day Passageway to Revival**, or even if you are praying alone, you will experience an enhanced intimacy with Christ, revival in your own life and an increased passion for social justice. As you enlarge your prayers to include revival in the life of your congregation, the Church of our Lord and for spiritual awakening among the citizens of your community, city, state/province and country, would you please consider using the 'crafted prayers' as a 'united launch' for your prayer? They are only provided as a suggested format and should not be allowed to hinder the Holy Spirit in directing your personal time of prayer in any fashion.

The New King James Version of the scriptures has been provided to aid the Holy Spirit in directing your prayers. Please read the entire reference during your personal prayer time and consider highlighting or underlining the scripture in your own Bible. Of course, you are welcome to use any other version of the Bible you may choose or are familiar with.

Please record any thoughts, scriptures, revelations, visions, or experiences that you may have during your prayer times.

Please keep a record of those people and circumstances which the Lord directs you to pray for.

Be sure to take time to be quiet before the Lord and allow Him an opportunity to speak to your mind and spirit.

You might use this **30-Day Passageway to Revival** booklet for several months to help you meditate on the various scriptures, and to allow the Holy Spirit to lead you into the truth of His heart for you in each of the areas mentioned. Some locations have used this for an extended '90 Day' effort in their churches and communities. Be flexible in the application and implementation of the principles of this writing.

PLEASE WRITE IN ADDITIONAL SCRIPTURES FROM YOUR OWN TIMES OF STUDY, MEDITATION AND PRAYER IN THE MANY LOCATIONS LEFT OPEN FOR YOU.

DAY 1

As you read and meditate on the following scriptures please pray for:

An intensified awareness of God's manifest (near) presence in your daily life.

Exodus 33:13-18 "'Now therefore, I pray, if I have found grace in Your sight, show me now Your way that I might know You and that I might find grace(*) in Your sight. And consider that this nation is Your people.' (14)And He (God) said, 'My Presence will go with you, and I will give you rest.' (15)Then he said to Him, 'If Your Presence does not go with us, do not take us up from here. (16)For how then will it be known that Your people and I have found grace in Your sight, except You go with us? So we shall be separate, Your people and I, from all the people who are upon the face of the earth.' (17)So the Lord said to Moses, 'I will also do this thing that you have spoken; for you have found grace in my sight, and I know you by name.' (18)And he (Moses) said, 'Please, show me Your glory.' "   *(*grace: undeserved and unreserved favor.)*

Deuteronomy 4:29 "But from there you will seek the LORD your God, and you will find Him if you seek Him with all your heart and with all your soul."

Job 42:5-6 "I have heard of You by the hearing of the ear, but now my eye sees You. (6)Therefore I abhor myself and repent in dust and ashes."

Psalms 84:1-2 "How lovely is Your tabernacle, O LORD of hosts! (2)My soul longs for, yes, even faints for the courts of the Lord; my heart and soul cry out for the living God."

Proverbs 3:6 "In all your ways acknowledge Him, and He shall direct your paths."

Other scriptures from your own study: _____

_____

A CRAFTED PRAYER

"Forgive me Lord for my satisfaction with knowing and experiencing so little of You in my everyday life.

Stir my heart to seek You with my whole heart and mind.

Open my eyes and my understanding to opportunities to acknowledge You in my life, as Your witness."

"WHAT'S GOD SAYING" during your reading and prayer time?

Notes:_____

_____

_____

_____

_____

_____

_____

_____

_____

List at least <u>one</u> person you can pray these scriptures for:

_____

"**ONE ANOTHER**" meditation for the day:

John 13:34-35 "A new commandment I give to you, that you love **one another**; as I have loved you, that you also love **one another**. (35)By this all will know that you are My disciples, if you have love for **one another**."

DAY 2

As you read and meditate on the following scriptures please pray for:

An acute sensitivity towards sin, (a pre-emptive, preventive sensitivity), in your own life and in the life of the community... a Holy Spirit revelation and redefinition of what constitutes 'sin.'

John 16:7-11 "Nevertheless I tell you the truth. It is to your advantage that I go away; for if I do not go away, the Helper will not come to you; but, if I depart, I will send Him to you. (8)And when He has come He will convict the world of sin, and of righteousness, and of judgment: (9)of sin, because they do not believe in Me; (10)of righteousness, because I go to My Father and you see Me no more; (11)of judgment, because the ruler of this world is judged."

Acts 17:29-31 "Therefore, since we are the offspring of God, we ought not to think that the Divine Nature is like gold or silver or stone, something shaped by art and man's devising. (30)Truly, these times of ignorance God overlooked, but now commands all men everywhere to repent, (31)because He has appointed a day on which He will judge the world in righteousness by the Man whom He has ordained. He has given assurance of this to all by raising Him from the dead."

Other scriptures from your own study: _____

_____

_____

_____

List at least <u>one</u> person you can pray these scriptures for:

_____

A CRAFTED PRAYER

"Dear Lord, please soften my callous heart where I have overlooked my sin and hardened my heart to Your instructions and warnings.

Help me to recognize what You consider to be displeasing in Your eyes according to Your Word.

Lead me by Your Spirit to change my definition of sin to match Yours."

"WHAT'S GOD SAYING" *during your reading and prayer time?*

Notes: _____

_____

_____

_____

_____

_____

_____

_____

"ONE ANOTHER" meditation for the day:

Romans 12:3-5 "For I say, through the grace given to me, to everyone who is among you, not to think of himself more highly than he ought to think, but to think soberly, as God has dealt to each one a measure of faith. [4]For as we have many members in one body, but all the members do not have the same function, [5]so we being many, are one body in Christ, and individually members of **one another**."

DAY 3

As you read and meditate on the following scriptures please pray for:

A jealous concern for the truth of God's written word in the Bible; and the display, declaration and demonstration of the gospel of the kingdom of God in an accurate, adequate and appropriate manner in every arena of our society and culture.

Psalms 119:9-16 "How can a young man cleanse his way? By taking heed to Your Word. (10)With my whole heart I have sought You; oh, let me not wander *(stray)* from Your commandments! (11)Your word I have hidden in my heart *(memorized)*, that I might not sin against You. (12)Blessed are You, O LORD! Teach me Your statutes. (13)With my lips I have declared all the judgments of Your mouth. (14)I have rejoiced in the way of Your testimonies, as much as in all riches. (15)I will meditate on Your precepts, and contemplate Your ways. (16)I will delight myself in Your statutes; I will not forget Your word."

Psalms 119:36-38 "Incline my heart to Your testimonies, and not to covetousness. (37)Turn away my eyes from looking at worthless things, and revive me in Your way. (38)Establish Your word to Your servant, who is devoted to fearing You."

Psalm 119:133, 136, 139 "Direct my steps by Your word, and let no iniquity have dominion over me. (136)Rivers of water run down from my eyes *(streams of tears)*, because men do not keep Your laws. (139)My zeal has consumed me, because my enemies have forgotten Your words."

Other scriptures from your own study: _____

_____

List at least <u>one</u> person you can pray these scriptures for:

_____

A CRAFTED PRAYER

"Dear Jesus, reveal to me, by Your Spirit, where my life does not line up with the 'plumbline' of Your word, the Bible, and Your Lordship.

Please help me to repent and turn away from every area of self-rule in my life.

Help me to know Your word more deeply, and to eagerly desire to submit to Your rule in every area of my life."

"WHAT'S GOD SAYING" during your reading and prayer time?

Notes:_____

_____

_____

_____

_____

_____

_____

_____

_____

"ONE ANOTHER" meditation for the day:

Romans 12:9-13 "Let love be without hypocrisy. Abhor what is evil. Cling to what is good. (10)Be kindly affectionate to **one another** with brotherly love, in honor giving preference to **one another**; (11)not lagging in diligence, fervent in spirit, serving the Lord; (12)rejoicing in hope, patient in tribulation, continuing steadfast in prayer; (13)distributing to the needs of the saints, given to hospitality."

DAY 4

As you read and meditate on the following scriptures please pray for:

An eagerness to hear and read the word of God as written in the Bible, and to hear and speak about the works of the Holy Spirit and our Lord... and a desperate, determined desire for and dependence upon the word of God.

Job 23:12 "I have not departed from the commandment of His lips; I have treasured the words of His mouth more than my necessary food."

Psalms 43:3-4 "Oh, send out Your light and Your truth! Let them lead me; let them bring me to Your holy hill and to Your tabernacle *(resting place).* (4)Then I will go to the altar of God, to God my exceeding joy; and on a harp I will praise You, O God, my God."

Psalms 119:105-108 "Your word is a lamp to my feet and a light to my path. (106)I have sworn and confirmed that I will keep Your righteous judgments. (107)I am afflicted very much; revive me, O LORD, according to Your word. (108)Accept, I pray, the free-will offerings of my mouth, O LORD, and teach me Your judgments."

Psalms 119:130-131 "The entrance of Your word gives light; it gives understanding to the simple. (131)I opened my mouth and panted, for I longed for Your commandments."

Psalms 119:161 "Princes persecute me without a cause, but my heart stands in awe of Your word. (162)I rejoice at Your word, as one who finds great treasure."

Other scriptures from your own study: _____

_____

_____

_____

A CRAFTED PRAYER

"Oh LORD, give me the grace to whole-heartedly believe that Your word is truth and must be the only 'plumbline' standard for my life.

Give me a desire and hunger for Your word that is stronger than for my daily bread."

"WHAT'S GOD SAYING" *during your reading and prayer time?*

Notes:_____

_____

_____

_____

_____

_____

_____

_____

_____

_____

List at least <u>one</u> person you can pray these scriptures for:

_____

"ONE ANOTHER" meditation for the day:

Romans 12:15-16 "Rejoice with those who rejoice, and weep with those who weep. (16)Be of the same mind toward **one another**. Do not set your mind on high things, but associate with the humble. Do not be wise in your own opinion."

DAY 5

As you read and meditate on the following scriptures please pray for:

An absorbing concern, concentration and commitment to intercessory prayer, praise, worship and fasting.

Psalms 5:1-3 "Give ear to my words, O LORD; consider my meditation. (2)Give heed to the voice of my cry, my King and my God, for to You will I pray; (3)my voice You shall hear in the morning, O LORD; in the morning I will direct it to You, and I will look up. (4)For You are not a God who takes pleasure in wickedness; nor shall evil dwell with You."

Psalms 119:145, 147-149 "I cry out with my whole heart; hear me, O LORD! I will keep Your statutes. (147)I rise before the dawning of the morning, and cry for help; I hope in Your word. (148)My eyes are awake through the night watches, that I may meditate on Your word. (149)Hear my voice according to Your loving-kindness; O LORD, revive me according to Your justice."

Ezekiel 22:30 "So I sought for a man among them who would make a wall, and stand in the gap before Me on behalf of the land, that I should not destroy it, but I found no one."

Matthew 26:40-41 "Then He came to the disciples and found them sleeping, and said to Peter, 'What? Could you not watch with Me one hour? (41)Watch and pray, lest you enter into temptation. The spirit indeed is willing, but the flesh is weak.' "

Other scriptures from your own study: _____

_____

_____

_____

A CRAFTED PRAYER

"Precious Lord Jesus, please increase my desire to spend more time in Your presence, enjoying You, adoring You and sharing my thoughts and concerns with You.

Help me establish a personal pattern of seeking You early in my day – everyday."

"WHAT'S GOD SAYING" *during your reading and prayer time?*

Notes:_____

_____

_____

_____

_____

_____

_____

_____

_____

_____

_____

List at least <u>one</u> person you can pray these scriptures for:

_____

"ONE ANOTHER" meditation for the day:

Romans 14:13 "Therefore let us not judge **one another** anymore, but rather resolve this, not to put a stumbling block or a cause to fall in our brother's way."

15

DAY 6

As you read and meditate on the following scriptures please pray for:

An enhanced standard of conduct and holiness in your own life and in the Church throughout the community.

Romans 6:18-22 "And having been set free from sin, you become slaves to righteousness. (19)I speak in human terms because of the weakness of your flesh. For just as you presented your members as slaves of uncleanness, and of lawlessness leading to more lawlessness, so now present your members as slaves of righteousness for holiness. (20)For when you were slaves to sin, you were free in regard to righteousness. (21)What fruit did you have then in the things which you are now ashamed? For the end of those things is death. (22)But now having been set free from sin, and having become slaves of God, you have your fruit to holiness, and the end, everlasting life."

2 Corinthians 7:1 "Therefore, having these promises, beloved, let us cleanse ourselves from all filthiness of the flesh and spirit, perfecting holiness in the fear of God."

Ephesians 4:17-20 "This I say, therefore, and testify in the Lord, that you should no longer walk as the rest of the Gentiles walk, in the futility of their minds, (18)having their understanding darkened, being alienated from the life of God, because of the ignorance that is in them, because of the blindness of their heart; (19)who, being past feeling have given themselves over to lewdness, to work all uncleanness with greediness. But you have not so learned Christ..." (Also read v. 21-32)

Other scriptures from your own study: _____

_____

_____

_____

A CRAFTED PRAYER

"Forgive me Lord where my life has not been a witness and a testimony to others of Your mercy, grace, righteousness and holy ways reigning in and through my life.

Cleanse and change my mind, motives and motions so that they will each glorify You and bring You pleasure."

"WHAT'S GOD SAYING" *during your reading and prayer time?*

Notes: _____

_____

_____

_____

_____

_____

_____

_____

_____

List at least <u>one</u> person you can pray these scriptures for:

_____

"ONE ANOTHER" meditation for the day:

Romans 15:5-7 "Now may the God of patience and comfort grant you to be like-minded toward **one another**, according to Christ Jesus, (6)that you may with one mind and one mouth glorify the God and Father of our Lord Jesus Christ. (7)Therefore receive **one another**, just as Christ also received us, to the glory of God."

DAY 7

As you read and meditate on the following scriptures please pray for:

A strengthening discernment of, concern for and loyalty towards the blood-bought Church of our Lord Jesus Christ among all its many and varied members.

Mark 9:38-40 "Now John answered Him, saying, 'Teacher, we saw someone who does not follow us casting out demons in Your name, and we forbade him because he does not follow us.' (39)But Jesus said, 'Do not forbid him, for no one who works a miracle in My name can soon afterward speak evil of Me. (40)For he who is not against us is on our side.' "

John 13:34-35 "A new commandment I give to you, that you love one another; as I have loved you, that you also love one another. (35)By this all men will know that you are My disciples."

John 17:20-22 "I do not pray for these alone, but also for those who will believe in Me through their word; (21)that they all may be one, as You Father, are in Me, and I in You; that they also may be one in Us, that the world may believe that You sent Me. (22)And the glory which You gave Me I have given them, that they may be one just as We are one."

Ephesians 2:19-21 "Now, therefore, you are no longer strangers and foreigners, but fellow citizens with the saints and members of the household of God, (20)having been built on the foundation of the apostles and prophets, Jesus Christ Himself being the chief cornerstone, (21)in whom the whole building, being fitted together, grows into a holy temple in the Lord..."

Other scriptures from your own study: _____

_____

18

A CRAFTED PRAYER

"My Father in heaven, show me where I have been an 'island' to myself, with little or no thought of how my life affects others.

Please increase my compassion, concern and care for the blood-bought body of Jesus Christ – His Church."

"WHAT'S GOD SAYING" *during your reading and prayer time?*

Notes:_____

_____

_____

_____

_____

_____

_____

_____

_____

_____

List at least <u>one</u> person you can pray these scriptures for:

_____

"ONE ANOTHER" meditation for the day:

<u>Romans 15:14</u> "Now I myself am confident concerning you, my brethren, that you also are full of goodness, filled with all knowledge, able also to admonish **one another**."

DAY 8

As you read and meditate on the following scriptures please pray for:

A growing realization and manifestation of unity in the purpose and motive of heart among Christians in the community; (PURPOSE: To bring Him pleasure, MOTIVE: For His great name's sake.)

Psalms 147:11 "The Lord takes pleasure (delights) in those who fear Him, in those who hope in His mercy."

Romans 15:1-6 "We then who are strong ought to bear with the scruples *(weaknesses)* of the weak, and not to please ourselves. (2)Let each of us please his neighbor for his good, leading to edification. (3)For even Christ did not please Himself, but as it is written, 'The reproaches of those who reproached You fell on Me.' (Psalm 69:9) (4)For whatever things were written before were written for our learning, that we through the patience and comfort of the scriptures might have hope. (5)Now may the God of patience and comfort grant you to be like-minded toward one another, according to Christ Jesus, (6)that you may with one mind and one mouth glorify the God and Father of our Lord Jesus Christ. (7)Therefore receive **one another**, just as Christ also received us, to the glory of God."

1 Corinthians 3:1-3 "And I, brethren, could not speak to you as to spiritual people but as to carnal, as to babes in Christ. (2)I fed you with milk and not with solid food; for until now you were not able to receive it, and even now you are still unable; (3)for you are still carnal. For where there are envy, strife and divisions among you, are you not carnal and behaving like mere men?"

Other scriptures from your own study: _____

_____

A CRAFTED PRAYER

"O Holy Spirit lead me into all truth, including a deeper revelation and understanding of what brings You pleasure and how I can please You by my attitudes and actions.

Please grant me a greater concern for how my attitudes and actions reflect upon Your name and reputation in the community where I live and work."

"WHAT'S GOD SAYING" *during your reading and prayer time?*

Notes: _____

_____

_____

_____

_____

_____

_____

_____

_____

_____

List at least <u>one</u> person you can pray these scriptures for:

_____

"ONE ANOTHER" meditation for the day:

Romans 13:8 "Owe no man anything except to love **one another**, for he who loves another has fulfilled the Law."

Romans 16:16 "Greet **one another** with a holy kiss. The churches of Christ greet you."

DAY 9

As you read and meditate on the following scriptures please pray for:

An increased zeal to <u>express</u> (present), <u>extend</u> (penetrate), <u>expand</u> (permeate) and <u>establish</u> (perpetuate) the kingdom of God through the evangelization and discipleship of a lost and dying Christ-rejecting world in the power of the Holy Spirit.

Psalms 119:136 "Rivers of water *(streams of tears)* run down from my eyes, because men do not keep your law."

Matthew 28:18-20 "And Jesus came and spoke to them, saying, 'All authority has been given to Me in heaven and on earth. (19)Go therefore and make disciples of all the nations, baptizing them in the name of the Father and of the Son and of the Holy Spirit, (20)teaching them to observe all things that I have commanded you; and lo, I am with you always, even to the end of the age.' Amen."

Mark 16:14-18 "Later He appeared to the eleven as they sat at the table; and He rebuked their unbelief and hardness of heart, because they did not believe those who had seen Him after He had risen. (15)And He said to them, 'Go into all the world and preach the gospel to every creature. (16)He who believes and is baptized will be saved; but he who does not believe will be condemned. (17)And these signs shall follow those who believe: In My name they will cast out demons; (18)they will speak with new tongues; they will take up serpents; and if they drink anything deadly, it will by no means hurt them; they will lay hands on the sick, and they will recover.' "

Other scriptures from your own study: _____

_____

_____

_____

A Crafted Prayer

My Lord and God, bring to life in me a deeper concern for the people throughout the whole world that I know are lost and without knowledge and experience of Your love and compassion for them, beginning with my family, neighbors and co-workers.

Please remind me to pray for them, and show me how to effectively reach out to them with the Good News of Your salvation and coming kingdom."

"__What's God saying__" during your reading and prayer time?

Notes: _____

_____

_____

_____

_____

_____

_____

List at least <u>one</u> person you can pray these scriptures for:

_____

"**One Another**" meditation for the day:

__John 13:14__ "If I then, your Lord and Teacher, have washed your feet, you also ought to wash **one another's** feet. For I have given you an example that you should do as I have done to you."

23

DAY 10

As you read and meditate on the following scriptures please pray for:

A passion for social justice based upon the Word of God.

Psalms 72:12-14 "For He will deliver the needy when he cries, the poor also, and him who has no helper. (13)He will spare the poor and the needy, and will save the souls of the needy. (14)He will redeem their life from oppression and violence; and precious shall be their blood in His sight."

Psalms 94:16 "Who will rise up for me against the evildoers? Who will stand up for me against the workers of iniquity?"

Psalms 103:6-10 "The Lord executes righteousness and justice for all who are oppressed. (7)He made known His ways to Moses, His acts to the children of Israel. (8)The Lord is merciful and gracious, slow to anger, and abounding in mercy. (9)He will not always strive with us. (10)He has not dealt with us according to our sins, nor punished us according to our iniquities."

Matthew 12:18-21 "Behold! My Servant whom I have chosen, My Beloved in whom My soul is well pleased! I will put My Spirit upon Him, and He will declare justice to the Gentiles. (19)He will not quarrel nor cry out; nor will anyone hear His voice in the streets. (20)A bruised reed He will not break, and smoking flax He will not quench, till He sends forth justice to victory; (21)and in His name Gentiles will trust."

Other scriptures from your own study: _____

_____

_____

List at least <u>one</u> person you can pray these scriptures for:

_____

A CRAFTED PRAYER

"By Your word Lord, reveal to me Your attitudes and expectations for righteousness and justice in Your world.

Cause my heart to be troubled by the unjust things that trouble and wound Your heart, and that are offensive to You, being contrary to the ways of Your kingdom."

"WHAT'S GOD SAYING" during your reading and prayer time?

Notes: _____

_____

_____

_____

_____

_____

_____

_____

_____

_____

"ONE ANOTHER" meditation for the day:

1 Corinthians 11:27-29, 33 "Therefore whoever eats this bread or drinks this cup of the Lord in an unworthy manner will be guilty of the body and the blood of the Lord. (28)But let a man examine himself, and so let him eat of the bread and drink of the cup. (29)For he who eats and drinks in an unworthy manner eats and drinks judgment to himself, not discerning the Lord's body. (33)Therefore, my brethren, when you come together to eat, wait for **one another**."

DAY 11

As you read and meditate on the following scriptures please pray for:

An intensified awareness of God's manifest (near) presence in your daily life.

Isaiah 26:7-9 "The way of the just is uprightness; O Most Upright! You weigh the path of the just. (8)Yes, in the ways of Your judgments, O LORD, we have waited for You; the desire of our soul is for Your name and for the remembrance of You. (9)With my soul I have desired You in the night, yes, by my spirit within me I will seek You early; for when Your judgments are in the earth, the inhabitants of the world will learn righteousness."

Jeremiah 29:11-13 "For I know the thoughts that I think toward you, says the LORD, thoughts of peace and not of evil, to give you a future and a hope. (12)Then you will call upon Me and go and pray to Me, and I will listen to you. (13)And you will seek Me and find Me, when you search for Me with all your heart."

Matthew 5:3-12 "Blessed are the poor in spirit, for theirs is the kingdom of heaven. (4)Blessed are those who mourn, for they shall be comforted. (5)Blessed are the meek, for they shall inherit the earth. (6)Blessed are those who hunger and thirst for righteousness, for they shall be filled. (7)Blessed are the merciful, for they shall obtain mercy. (8)Blessed are the pure in heart, for they shall see God. (9)Blessed are the peacemakers, for they shall be called sons of God. (10)Blessed are those who are persecuted for righteousness sake, for theirs is the kingdom of heaven. (11)Blessed are you when they revile and persecute you, and say all kinds of evil against you falsely for My sake. (12)Rejoice and be exceedingly glad..."

Other scriptures from your own study: _____

_____

A CRAFTED PRAYER

"Show us Lord, how to experience a greater degree of Your presence in our community of believers, in our study of Your holy word and during our earnest prayer times with each other.

Become our hearts' 'great desire,' O Lord! "

"WHAT'S GOD SAYING" *during your reading and prayer time?*

Notes: _____

_____

_____

_____

_____

_____

_____

List at least <u>one</u> person you can pray these scriptures for:

_____

"ONE ANOTHER" meditation for the day:

1 Corinthians 12:24(b)-27 "…but God composed the body, having given greater honor to that part which lacks it, (25)that there should be no schism in the body; but that the members should have the same care for **one another**. (26)And if one member suffers, all the members suffer with it; or if one member is honored, all the members rejoice with it. (27)Now you are the body of Christ, and members individually."

DAY 12

As you read and meditate on the following scriptures please pray for:

An acute sensitivity towards sin, (a pre-emptive, preventive sensitivity), in your own life and in the life of the community... a Holy Spirit revelation and redefinition of what constitutes 'sin.'

1 Peter 4:1-3 "Therefore, since Christ suffered for us in the flesh, arm yourselves also with the same mind, for he who has suffered in the flesh has ceased from sin, (2)that he no longer should live the rest of his time in the lust of men, but for the will of God. (3)For we have spent enough of our past lifetime in doing the will of the gentiles, when we walked in lewdness, lusts, drunkenness, revelries, drinking parties, and abominable idolatries."

1 Peter 4:17-18 "For the time has come for judgment to begin at the house of God; and if it begins with us first, what will be the end of those who do not obey the gospel of God. (18)Now, 'If the righteous one is scarcely saved, where will the ungodly and the sinner appear?' "

(Proverbs 11:31)

1 John 1:8-10 "If we say that we have no sin, we deceive ourselves, and the truth is not in us. (9)If we confess our sins, He is faithful and just to forgive us our sins and to cleanse us from all unrighteousness. (10)If we say that we have not sinned, we make Him a liar, and His Word is not in us."

Other scriptures from your own study: _____

_____

_____

List at least <u>one</u> person you can pray these scriptures for:

_____

A CRAFTED PRAYER

"Thank You Father for Your mercy and forgiveness of our sin as we confess our faults to You.

Please make us more sensitive to the leading of Your Spirit in obedience to Your word, that we might not sin against You in public or in private.

Increase our desire to please You in our day-to-day lives; as You search our hearts may You be pleased."

"WHAT'S GOD SAYING" *during your reading and prayer time?*

Notes: _____

_____

_____

_____

_____

_____

_____

_____

_____

"ONE ANOTHER" meditation for the day:

1 Peter 4:7-10 "But the end of all things is at hand, therefore be serious and watchful in your prayers. (8)And above all things have fervent love for **one another**, for 'love will cover a multitude of sins.' (9)Be hospitable to **one another**, without grumbling. (10)As each one has received a gift, minister it to **one another**, as good stewards of the manifold grace of God."

Day 13

As you read and meditate on the following scriptures please pray for:

A jealous concern for the truth of God's written word in the Bible; and the display, declaration and demonstration of the gospel of the kingdom of God in an accurate, adequate and appropriate manner in every arena of our society and culture.

Psalm 119:106-107 "I have sworn and confirmed that I will keep Your righteous judgments. (107)I am afflicted very much; revive me, O LORD, according to Your Word."

Psalm 119:111-112 "Your testimonies I have taken as a heritage *(inheritance)* forever, for they are the rejoicing of my heart. (112)I have inclined my heart to perform Your statutes forever, to the very end."

Psalm 119:126-128 "It is time for You to act, O LORD, for they have regarded Your law as void. (127)Therefore I love Your commandments more than gold, yes, than fine gold! (128)Therefore all You precepts concerning all things I consider to be right; I hate every false way *(wrong path)*."

Psalm 145:10-13 "All Your works shall praise You, O Lord, and Your saints shall bless You. (11)They shall speak of the glory of Your kingdom, and talk of Your power, (12)to make known to the sons of men His mighty acts, and the glorious majesty of His kingdom. (13)Your kingdom is an everlasting kingdom, and Your dominion endures throughout all generations."

Other scriptures from your own study: _____

_____

_____

List at least <u>one</u> person you can pray these scriptures for:

_____

A CRAFTED PRAYER

"Dear God, please change our hearts, attitudes and actions towards Your commandments.

May we seek to obey Your laws, not grudgingly or reluctantly, but eagerly out of our loving response and devotion to You and commitment to the ways of Your kingdom."

"WHAT'S GOD SAYING" *during your reading and prayer time?*

Notes:_____

_____

_____

_____

_____

_____

_____

_____

_____

_____

"**ONE ANOTHER**" meditation for the day:

Galatians 5:13-14 "For you, brethren, have been called in liberty; only do not use liberty as an opportunity for the flesh, but through love serve **one another**. (14)For all of the law is fulfilled in one word, even in this: *'You shall love your neighbor as yourself.'* "   *(Leviticus 19:18)*

DAY 14

As you read and meditate on the following scriptures please pray for:

An eagerness to hear and read the word of God as written in the Bible, and to hear and speak about the works of the Holy Spirit and our Lord... and a desperate, determined desire for and dependence upon the word of God.

Psalms 119:165-169 "Great peace have those who love Your law, and nothing causes them to stumble. (166)LORD, I hope for Your salvation, and I do Your commandments. (167)My soul keeps Your testimonies, and I love them exceedingly. (169)I keep Your precepts and Your testimonies, for all my ways are before You. (169)Let my cry come before You, O Lord; give me understanding according to Your word."

Isaiah 66:2 " 'For all those things My hand has made, and all those things exist,' says the LORD. 'But on this one will I look: on him who is poor and of a contrite spirit, and who trembles at My word' "

Mark 4:24-25 "Then He said to them, 'Take heed what you hear. With the same measure you use it will be measured to you; and to you who hear, more will be given. (25)For whoever has, to him more will be given; but whoever does not have, even what he has will be taken away from him.'"

Luke 24:32 "And they said to one another, 'Did not our heart burn within us while He talked with us on the road, and while He opened the Scriptures to us?' "

Luke 24:45 "And He opened their understanding that they might comprehend the scriptures."

Other scriptures from your own study: _____

_____

_____

A CRAFTED PRAYER

"Holy Spirit, help us as a congregation to so hunger for Your instruction in the truth of Your word and the ways of Your kingdom, that we will not be able to leave our homes at the start of our day without seeking You to feed us from Your word, as written in the Bible."

---

*"**WHAT'S GOD SAYING**" during your reading and prayer time?*

Notes: _____

_____

_____

_____

_____

_____

_____

_____

_____

_____

List at least <u>one</u> person you can pray these scriptures for:

_____

"**ONE ANOTHER**" meditation for the day:

Galatians 6:1-2 "Brethren, if a man is overtaken in any trespass, you who are spiritual restore such a one in a spirit of gentleness, considering yourself lest you also be tempted. (2)Bear **one another's** burdens, and so fulfill the law of Christ."

DAY 15

As you read and meditate on the following scriptures please pray for:

An absorbing concern, concentration and commitment to intercessory prayer, praise, worship and fasting.

Luke 18:1 "Then He spoke a parable to them that men always ought to pray and not lose heart."

Luke 22:40, 46 "When He came to the place, He said to them, 'Pray that you may not enter into temptation.' (46)Then He said to them, 'Why do you sleep? Rise and pray, lest you enter into temptation.' "

Romans 8:26-27 "Likewise the Spirit also helps in our weaknesses. For we do not know what we should pray for as we ought, but the Spirit Himself makes intercession for us with groanings which cannot be uttered. (27)Now He who searches the hearts knows what the mind of the Spirit is, because He makes intercession for the saints according to the will of God."

1 Corinthians 2:9-11 "But as it is written: 'Eye has not seen, nor ear heard, nor have entered into the heart of man the things which God has prepared for those who love Him.' (10)But God has revealed them to us through His Spirit. For the Spirit searches all things, yes, the deep things of God. (11)For what man knows the things of a man except the spirit of the man which is in him. Even so no one knows the things of God except the Spirit of God."

1 Corinthians 2:16 "For *'who has known the mind of the LORD that he may instruct Him?'* But we have the mind of Christ."

Other scriptures from your own study: _____

_____

A CRAFTED PRAYER

"Holy Spirit instruct Your Church how to fast and pray in a manner that is effective, and heighten our sensitivity to Your instruction and direction as we deny the desires of the flesh.

Reveal to us the burdens that are on Your heart which we can lift to You in 'partnership prayer' today."

"WHAT'S GOD SAYING" *during your reading and prayer time?*

Notes: _____

_____

_____

_____

_____

_____

_____

_____

_____

_____

List at least <u>one</u> person you can pray these scriptures for:

_____

"ONE ANOTHER" meditation for the day:

Ephesians 4:31-32 "Let all bitterness, wrath, anger, clamor and evil speaking be put away from you, with all malice. (32)And be kind to **one another**, tenderhearted, forgiving **one another**, even as God in Christ forgave you."

DAY 16

An enhanced standard of conduct and holiness in your own life and in the Church throughout the community.

Ephesians 4:29 "Let no corrupt word proceed out of your mouth, but what is good for necessary edification, that it may impart grace to the hearers.

Ephesians 5:1-5 "Therefore be imitators of God as dear children. (2)And walk in love, as Christ also has given Himself for us, an offering and a sacrifice to God for a sweet smelling aroma. (3)But fornication and all uncleanness or covetousness, let it not even be named among you, as is fitting for saints; (4)neither filthiness, nor foolish talking, nor course jesting, which are not fitting, but rather giving of thanks. (5)For this you know, that no fornicator, unclean person, nor covetous man, who is an idolater, has any inheritance in the kingdom of Christ and God." *(Also read verses 6-21.)*

Colossians 3:5-10 "Therefore put to death your members which are on the earth: fornication, uncleanness, passion, evil desire, and covetousness, which is idolatry. (6)Because of these things the wrath of God is coming upon the sons of disobedience, (7)in which you yourselves once walked when you lived in them. (8)But now you yourselves are to put off all these: anger, wrath, malice, blasphemy, filthy language out of your mouth. (9)Do not lie to one another, since you have put off the old man with his deeds (10)and have put on the new man who is renewed in knowledge according to the image of Him who created him..."

Other scriptures from your own study: _____

_____

A CRAFTED PRAYER

"Convict us Holy Spirit of the sins we commit with the words of our mouth, and the motives of our hearts behind those words.

May our conversation be fitting and pleasing as children of the King of Glory, imparting grace to those who are listening according to their needs."

"WHAT'S GOD SAYING" *during your reading and prayer time?*

Notes: _____

_____

_____

_____

_____

_____

_____

_____

List at least <u>one</u> person you can pray these scriptures for:

_____

"ONE ANOTHER" meditation for the day:

Colossians 3:12-13 "Therefore, as the elect of God, holy and beloved, put on tender mercies, kindness, humility, meekness, longsuffering; (13)bearing with **one another**, and forgiving **one another**, if anyone has a complaint against another; even as Christ forgave you, so you also must do."

37

DAY 17

As you read and meditate on the following scriptures please pray for:

A strengthening discernment of, concern for and loyalty towards the blood-bought Church of our Lord Jesus Christ among all its members.

Romans 12:4-5 "For as we have many members in one body, but all the members do not have the same function, (5)so we, being many, are one body in Christ, and individually members of **one another**."

Romans 12:9-13 "Let love be without hypocrisy. Abhor what is evil. Cling to what is good. (10)Be kindly affectionate to **one another** with brotherly love, in honor giving preference to **one another**; (11)not lagging in diligence, fervent in spirit, serving the Lord; (12)rejoicing in hope, patient in tribulation, continuing steadfastly in prayer; (13)distributing to the needs of the saints, given to hospitality."

Hebrews 10:24-25 "And let us consider **one another** in order to stir up love and good works, (25)not forsaking the assembling of ourselves together, as is the manner of some, but exhorting **one another** as you see the Day approaching."

1 Peter 4:8-9 "And above all things have fervent love for **one another**, for 'love will cover a multitude of sins.' (9)Be hospitable to **one another** without grumbling."

Other scriptures from your own study: _____

_____

_____

List at least <u>one</u> person you can pray these scriptures for:

_____

A CRAFTED PRAYER

"Oh Father, in our community of believers please help us to recognize and appreciate the unique gifts and functions You have given to each one of us in order for our entire Church fellowship to be built up and strengthened in You.

Show us how to walk and work together in harmony, giving us the grace to be faithful to pray for each other regularly as an expression of our love."

*"**WHAT'S GOD SAYING**" during your reading and prayer time?*

Notes: _____

_____

_____

_____

_____

_____

_____

_____

_____

"**ONE ANOTHER**" meditation for the day:

1 Thessalonians 3:12-13   "And may the Lord make you increase and abound in love to **one another** and to all, just as we do to you, (13)so that He may establish your hearts blameless in holiness before our God and Father at the coming of our Lord Jesus Christ with all His saints."

DAY 18

As you read and meditate on the following scriptures please pray for:

A growing realization and manifestation of unity in the purpose and motive of heart among Christians in the community; (PURPOSE: To bring Him pleasure, MOTIVE: For His great name's sake.)

Galatians 5:24-26 "And those who are Christ's have crucified the flesh with its passions and desires. (25)If we live in the Spirit, let us also walk in the Spirit. (26)Let us not become conceited, provoking **one another**, envying **one another**."

Galatians 6:2 "Bear **one another's** burdens, and so fulfill the law of Christ."

Philippians 2:1-4 "Therefore if there is any consolation in Christ, if any comfort of love, if any fellowship of the Spirit, if any affection and mercy, (2)fulfill my joy by being like-minded, having the same love, being of one accord, of one mind. (3)Let nothing be done through selfish ambition or conceit, but in lowliness of mind let each esteem others better than himself. (4)Let each of you look out not only for his own interests, but also for the interests of others."

Revelation 4:11 (KJV) "Thou art worthy, O LORD, to receive glory and honor and power: for thou hast created all things, and for Thy pleasure they are and were created."

Other scriptures from your own study: _____

_____

_____

List at least <u>one</u> person you can pray these scriptures for:

_____

A CRAFTED PRAYER

"Holy Spirit, search out and reveal to us our inner motives such as pride, jealousy, selfish ambition and sense of entitlement which displease You and cause dissension among Your body of believers and disciples.

Change our hearts so we can reflect Your glory in the community where we live, work and attend school."

"WHAT'S GOD SAYING" *during your reading and prayer time?*

Notes: _____

_____

_____

_____

_____

_____

_____

_____

_____

_____

"ONE ANOTHER" meditation for the day:

1 Thessalonians 4:16-18 "For the Lord Himself will descend from heaven with a shout, with the voice of an archangel, and with the trumpet of God. And the dead in Christ will rise first. (17)Then we who are alive and remain shall be caught up together with them in the clouds to meet the Lord in the air. And thus we shall always be with the Lord. (18)Therefore comfort **one another** with these words."

41

DAY 19

As you read and meditate on the following scriptures please pray for:

An increased zeal to <u>express</u> (present), <u>extend</u> (penetrate), <u>expand</u> (permeate) and <u>establish</u> (perpetuate) the kingdom of God through the evangelization and discipleship of a lost and dying Christ-rejecting world in the power of the Holy Spirit.

Matthew 6:9-10 ""In this manner, therefore, pray: Our Father in heaven, hallowed be Your name. (10)Your kingdom come. Your will be done on earth as it is in heaven."

Matthew 6:33 "But seek first the kingdom of God and His righteousness, and all these things shall be added to you."

Matthew 24:14 "And this gospel of the kingdom will be preached in all the world as a witness to all nations, and then the end will come."

Luke 12:31-32 "But seek the kingdom of God, and all these things shall be added to you. (32)Do not fear, little flock, for it is your Father's good pleasure to give you the kingdom."

Romans 14:16-19 "Therefore do not let your good be spoken of as evil; (17)for the kingdom of God is not eating and drinking, but righteousness and peace and joy in the Holy Spirit. (18)For he who serves Christ in these things is acceptable to God and approved by men. **(19)**Therefore let us pursue (make every effort to attain) the things which make for peace and the things by which one may edify another. "

Other scriptures from your own study: _____

_____

A CRAFTED PRAYER

"Lord Jesus, may our minds, hearts and emotions' deep desire be to see You lifted up and obeyed as King of all levels of society, culture, government and spiritual life, both here and among all the nations of the earth."

"WHAT'S GOD SAYING" *during your reading and prayer time?*

Notes: _____

_____

_____

_____

_____

_____

_____

_____

_____

List at least <u>one</u> person you can pray these scriptures for:

_____

"ONE ANOTHER" meditation for the day:

1 Thessalonians 5:9-11 "For God did not appoint us to wrath, but to obtain salvation through our Lord Jesus Christ, (10)who died for us, that whether we wake or sleep, we should live together with Him. (11)Therefore comfort **each other** and edify **one another**, just as you are also doing."

DAY 20

As you read and meditate on the following scriptures please pray for:

A passion for social justice based upon the Word of God.

Psalm 94:20-21 "Shall the throne of iniquity, which devises evil by law, have fellowship with You? They gather together against the life of the righteous, and condemn innocent blood."

Psalm 101:1-8 "I will sing of mercy and justice; To You O LORD, I will sing praises. (2)I will behave wisely in a perfect way. Oh, when will You come to me? I will walk within my house with a perfect heart. (3)I will set nothing wicked before my eyes; I hate the work of those who fall away; it will not cling to me. (4)A perverse heart shall depart from me; I will not know wickedness. (5)Whoever secretly slanders his neighbor, him will I destroy; the proud one who has a haughty look and a proud heart, him I will not endure. (6)My eyes shall be on the faithful of the land, that they may dwell with me; he who walks in a perfect way, he shall serve me. (7)He who works deceit shall not dwell within my house; he who tells lies shall not continue in my presence. (8)Early I will destroy all the wicked of the land, that I may cut off all the evildoers from the city of the LORD."

Isaiah 42:21-22 "The LORD is well pleased for His righteousness' sake; He will exalt the law and make it honorable. (22)But this is a people robbed and plundered; all of them are snared in holes, and they are hidden in prison houses; they are for prey, and no one delivers *(rescues them)*; for plunder, and no one says, 'Restore *(send them back).*' "

Other scriptures from your own study: _____

_____

44

A CRAFTED PRAYER

"Almighty God, stir our hearts to mourning and our hands and feet to action when Your laws are ignored, rejected, despised and perverted by law-makers and our courts.

God of mercy, move by Your Spirit upon the law-makers and justices of the nation to ban the practice of abortion and restore the Ten Commandments as a moral and ethical foundational basis of our culture and society."

"WHAT'S GOD SAYING" *during your reading and prayer time?*

Notes: _____

_____

_____

_____

_____

_____

List at least <u>one</u> person you can pray these scriptures for:

_____

"ONE ANOTHER" meditation for the day:

Hebrews 10:23-25 "Let us hold fast the confession of our faith, for He who promised is faithful. (24)And let us consider **one another** in order to stir up love and good works, (25)not forsaking the assembling of ourselves together, as is the manner of some, but exhorting **one another**, and so much the more as you see the Day approaching."

45

DAY 21

As you read and meditate on the following scriptures please pray for:

An intensified awareness of God's manifest nearness and presence in your daily life.

Hosea 6:1-3 "Come and let us return to the Lord; for He has torn, but He will heal us; He has stricken, but He will bind us up. (2)After two days He will revive us; on the third day He will raise us up, that we may live in His sight. (3)Let us know, let us pursue the knowledge of the Lord. ("Let us press on to acknowledge Him." [NIV]) His going forth is established as the morning: He will come to us like the rain, like the latter and former rain to the earth."

Matthew 5:8-9 "Blessed are the pure of heart, for they shall see God. (9)Blessed are the peacemakers, for they shall be called sons of God."

John 15:14-17 "You are my friends if you do what I command you. (15)No longer do I call you servants, for a servant does not know what his master is doing; but I have called you friends, for all things that I heard from My Father I have made known to you. (16)You did not choose Me, but I chose you and appointed you that you should go and bear fruit, and that your fruit should remain *(endure, multiply)*, that whatever you ask the Father in My name He may give you. (17)These things I command you, that you love one another."

Hebrews 11:6 "But without faith it is impossible to please Him, for he who comes to God must believe that He is, and that He is the rewarder of those who diligently seek Him."

Other scriptures from your own study: _____

_____

_____

46

A Crafted Prayer

"Jesus, You have called us 'friends,' and yet we so often fail to acknowledge You, even as we would a close friend walking at our side, or during a conversation.

Please forgive us and show us how to turn to You constantly, seeking Your opinion, Your direction and Your strength for every decision and in every possible situation and opportunity that we encounter in our lives."

*"**What's God saying**" during your reading and prayer time?*

Notes: _____

_____

_____

_____

_____

_____

_____

_____

List at least <u>one</u> person you can pray these scriptures for:

_____

"**One Another**" meditation for the day:

James 4:11-12 "Do not speak evil of **one another**, brethren. He who speaks evil of a brother and judges his brother, speaks evil of the law and judges the law. But if you judge the law, you are not a doer of the law but a judge. (12)There is one Lawgiver, who is able to save and destroy. Who are you to judge **another**?"

47

DAY 22

As you read and meditate on the following scriptures please pray for:

An acute sensitivity towards sin, (a pre-emptive, preventive sensitivity), in your own life and in the life of the community... a Holy Spirit revelation and redefinition of what constitutes 'sin.'

Psalm 101:1-3 "I will sing of mercy and justice; to You, O LORD, I will sing praises. (2)I will behave wisely in a perfect way. Oh, when will You come to me? I will walk within my house with a perfect heart. (3)I will set nothing wicked before my eyes; I hate the work of those who fall away; it shall not cling to me."

Ephesians 4:25-30 "Therefore, putting away lying, *'let each one of you speak truth with his neighbor,'* for we are members of **one another**. (26)*'Be angry and do not sin':* do not let the sun go down on your wrath, (27)nor give place to the devil. (29)Let him who stole steal no longer, but rather let him labor, working with his hands what is good, that he may have something to give him who has need. (29)Let no corrupt word proceed out of your mouth, but what is good for necessary edification, that it might impart grace to the hearers. (30)And do not grieve the Holy Spirit of God, by whom you were sealed for the day of redemption."

James 4:17 "Therefore, to him who knows to do good and does not do it, to him it is sin."

Other scriptures from your own study: _____

_____

_____

_____

_____

A CRAFTED PRAYER

"Lord, give us a hunger and zeal to walk before You in a 'perfect way,' even when no one but You can see us, in order that we might please You in the attitudes of our hearts, our speech, our actions and our deeds.

Open our eyes to see how we grieve You by failing to do the good that we know we should do, and to show Your love to the world in the manner You have commanded."

WHAT'S GOD SAYING" *during your reading and prayer time?*

Notes: _____

_____

_____

_____

_____

_____

List at least <u>one</u> person you can pray these scriptures for:

_____

"ONE ANOTHER" meditation for the day:

Ephesians 5:18-21 "And do not be drunk with wine, in which is dissipation; but be filled with the Spirit, (19)speaking to **one another** in psalms and hymns and spiritual songs, singing and making melody in your heart to the Lord, (20)giving thanks always for all things to God the Father, in the name of our Lord Jesus Christ, (21)submitting to **one another** in the fear of God."

DAY 23

As you read and meditate on the following scriptures please pray for:

A jealous concern for the truth of God's written word in the Bible; and the display, declaration and demonstration of the gospel of the kingdom of God in an accurate, adequate and appropriate manner in every arena of our society and culture.

Matthew 24:14 "And this gospel of the kingdom will be preached in all the world as a witness to all the nations, and then the end will come."

1 Timothy 6:3-5 "If anyone teaches otherwise and does not consent to wholesome words, even the words of our Lord Jesus Christ, and to the doctrine which accords with godliness, (4)he is proud, knowing nothing, but is obsessed with disputes and arguments over words, from which come envy, strife, reviling, evil suspicions, (5)useless wrangling's of men of corrupt minds and destitute of the truth, who suppose that godliness is a means of gain. From such withdraw yourself."

2 Timothy 2:14-15 "Remind them of these things, charging them before the Lord not to strive about words to no profit, to the ruin of the hearers. (15)Be diligent to present yourself approved to God, a worker who does not need to be ashamed, rightly dividing the Word of truth."

2 Timothy 3:16-17 "All scripture is given by inspiration of God, and is profitable for doctrine, for reproof, for correction, for instruction in righteousness, (17)that the man of God may be complete, thoroughly equipped for every good work."

Other scriptures from your own study: _____

_____

_____

A CRAFTED PRAYER

"O Lord, how we love Your word, and we praise You that it is able to actively penetrate from the darkest hidden places of our hearts, to the highest points of society.

Teach us how to handle Your word as skillful workmen, approved by You, to reach our entire broken, dysfunctional world with Your incredible love, mercy and justice."

"WHAT'S GOD SAYING" *during your reading and prayer time?*

Notes: _____

_____

_____

_____

_____

_____

_____

_____

List at least <u>one</u> person you can pray these scriptures for:

_____

"ONE ANOTHER" meditation for the day:

1 John 3:10-11 "In this the children of God and the children of the devil are manifest: whoever does not practice righteousness is not of God, nor is he who does not love his brother. (11)For this is the message that you heard from the beginning, that we should love **one another**..."

DAY 24

As you read and meditate on the following scriptures please pray for:

An eagerness to hear and read the word of God as written in the Bible, and to hear and speak about the works of the Holy Spirit and our Lord... and a desperate, determined desire for and dependence upon the word of God.

Mark 4:24-25 "Then He said to them, 'Take heed what you hear. With the same measure you use, it will be measured to you; and to you who hear, more will be given. (25)For whoever has, to him more will be given; but whoever does not have, even what he has will be taken away from him.'"

Luke 8:16-18 "No one, when he has lit a lamp, covers it with a vessel or puts it under a bed, but sets it on a lampstand, that those who enter may see the light. (17)For nothing is secret that will not be revealed, nor anything hidden that will not be known and come to light. (18)Therefore take heed how you hear. For whoever has, to him more will be given; and whoever does not have, even what he seems to have will be taken from him."

John 8:31-32 "Then Jesus said to those Jews who believed Him, 'If you abide in My Word, you are my disciples indeed. (32)And you shall know the truth, and the truth shall make you free.'"

Romans 10:17 "So then faith comes by hearing, and hearing by the word of God."

Other scriptures from your own study: _____

_____

_____

_____

_____

A CRAFTED PRAYER

"We need your strength O LORD, for our society and media offer such enticing and entertaining alternatives to the hearing, reading and appropriate sharing of Your Word.

Give us the courage to put these distractions aside more often so we can seek You in Your word with increased eagerness, attentiveness, obedience and joy, for Your great name's sake, as a witness of Your worthiness."

"WHAT'S GOD SAYING" during your reading and prayer time?

Notes:_____

_____

_____

_____

_____

_____

_____

List at least <u>one</u> person you can pray these scriptures for:

_____

"ONE ANOTHER" meditation for the day:

Colossians 3:14-17 "But above all these things put on love, which is the bond of perfection. (15)And let the peace of God rule in your hearts, to which also you were called in one body; and be thankful. (16)Let the word of Christ dwell in you richly in all wisdom, teaching and admonishing **one another** is psalms and hymns and spiritual songs, singing with grace in your hearts to the Lord."

DAY 25

As you read and meditate on the following scriptures please pray for:

An absorbing concern, concentration and commitment to intercessory prayer, praise, worship and fasting.

Romans 8:26-27 "Likewise the Spirit also helps in our weaknesses. For we do not know what we should pray for as we ought, but the Spirit Himself makes intercession for us with groanings which cannot be uttered. (27)Now He who searches the hearts knows what the mind of the Spirit is because He makes intercession according to the will of God."

Ephesians 6:18 "Praying always with all prayer and supplication in the Spirit, being watchful to this end with all perseverance and supplication for all the saints..."

1 Timothy 2:1-2 "Therefore I exhort first of all that supplications, prayers, intercessions and giving of thanks be made for all men, (2)for kings and all who are in authority, that we may lead a quiet and peaceable life in all godliness and reverence."

2 Timothy 1:6-7 "Therefore I remind you to stir up the gift of God which is in you through the laying on of my hands. (7)For God has not given us a spirit of fear, but of power and of love and of a sound mind."

1 Peter 4:7 "But the end of all things is at hand; therefore be serious and watchful in your prayers."

Jude 20 "But you, beloved, building yourselves up on your most holy faith, praying in the Holy Spirit, keep yourselves in the love of God, looking for the mercy of our Lord Jesus Christ unto eternal life."

Other scriptures from your own study: _____

_____

A CRAFTED PRAYER

"Precious Lord, fan the flame of our love for You. Help us, like the five wise virgins of Matthew 25:1-13, to watch faithfully and eagerly for Your return, being careful to maintain the presence of the Holy Spirit in our lives.

At Your throne may we find that new song of intimate adoration, fellowship and worship; and take up the scepter of Your kingdom power in mighty, effective intercession and justifiable spiritual warfare."

"WHAT'S GOD SAYING" *during your reading and prayer time?*

Notes:_____

_____

_____

_____

_____

_____

_____

_____

List at least <u>one</u> person you can pray these scriptures for:

_____

"ONE ANOTHER" meditation for the day:

James 5:16 "Confess your trespasses *(faults, sins)* to **one another**, and pray for **one another**, that you may be healed. The effective, fervent prayer of a righteous man *(on behalf of another)* avails much."

DAY 26

As you read and meditate on the following scriptures please pray for:

An enhanced standard of conduct and holiness in your own life and in the Church throughout the community.

2 Thessalonians 3:5 "Now may the Lord direct your hearts into the love of God and into the patience of Christ."

Hebrews 12:10, 14 "For they *(our fathers)* indeed for a few days chastened us as seemed best to them, but He for our profit, that we might be partakers of His holiness." (14)"Pursue peace with all people, and holiness, without which no one will see the Lord."

James 1:19-22 "So then my beloved brethren, let every man be swift to hear, slow to speak, slow to wrath; (20)for the wrath of man does not produce the righteousness of God. (21)Therefore lay aside all filthiness and overflow of wickedness, and receive with meekness the implanted word, which is able to save your souls. (22)But be doers of the word, and not hearers only, deceiving yourselves."

1 Peter 1:15-17 "But as He who called you is holy, you also be holy in all your conduct, (16)because it is written, *'Be holy, for I am holy.'* (17)And if you call on the Father, who without partiality judges according to each one's work, conduct yourselves throughout the time of your stay in fear;"

1 Peter 1:22-23 "Since you have purified your souls in obeying the truth through the Spirit in sincere love of the brethren, love **one another** fervently with a pure heart, (23)having been born again, not of corruptible seed but incorruptible, through the word of God which lives and abides forever..."

Other scriptures from your own study: _____

_____

A CRAFTED PRAYER

"Lord Jesus, please purify our hearts, mouths and lives that our community may see the distinction between the righteous and the wicked, between those who serve the true and living God and those who do not. (Malachi 3:18)

Help us to boldly stand up for Your righteousness and justice in our community, city and our country."

"WHAT'S GOD SAYING" *during your reading and prayer time?*

Notes: _____

_____

_____

_____

_____

_____

_____

List at least <u>one</u> person you can pray these scriptures for:

_____

"ONE ANOTHER" meditation for the day:

1 Peter 5:5-7 "Likewise you younger people, submit yourselves to your elders. Yes, all of you be submissive to **one another**, and be clothed in humility, for 'God resists the proud, but gives grace to the humble.' (6)Therefore humble yourselves under the mighty hand of God, that He may exalt you in due time, (7)casting all your cares upon Him, for He cares for you."

57

DAY 27

As you read and meditate on the following scriptures please pray for:

A strengthening discernment of, concern for and loyalty towards the blood-bought Church of our Lord Jesus Christ among all its members.

1 Corinthians 12:12-14 "For as the body is one and has many members, but all the members of that one body, being many, are one body, so also is Christ. (13)For by one Spirit we were all baptized into one body – whether Jews or Greeks, whether slaves or free – and have all been made to drink into one Spirit. (14)For in fact the body is not one member but many."

1 Corinthians 12:18-21(a) "But now God has set the members, each one of them, in the body just as He pleased. (19)And if they were all one member, where would the body be? (20)But now indeed there are many members, yet one body. (21)And the eye cannot say to the hand, 'I have no need of you'..."

Galatians 3:26-29 "For you are all sons of God through faith in Christ Jesus. (27)For as many of you as were baptized into Christ have put on Christ. (28)There is neither Jew nor Greek, there is neither slave nor free, there is neither male nor female; for you are all one in Christ Jesus. (29)And if you are Christ's, then you are Abraham's seed, and heirs according to the promise."

Hebrews 13:3 "Remember the prisoners as if chained with them – those who are mistreated – since you yourselves are in the body also."

Other scriptures from your own study: _____

_____

_____

A CRAFTED PRAYER

"Lord, we seek You for a clearer vision and a greater compassion for Your Church in our community and throughout the earth, so we may more faithfully pray, give, support, encourage, fellowship with and build up Your Body, the Church, worldwide for Your end-time purposes."

"WHAT'S GOD SAYING" *during your reading and prayer time?*

Notes: _____

_____

_____

_____

_____

_____

_____

List at least <u>one</u> person you can pray these scriptures for:

_____

"ONE ANOTHER" meditation for the day:

1 John 1:5-7 "This is the message which we have heard from Him and declare to you, that God is light and in Him is no darkness at all. (6)If we say that we have fellowship with Him, and walk in darkness, we lie and do not practice the truth. (7)But if we walk in the light as He is in the light, we have fellowship with **one another**. And the blood of Jesus Christ His Son cleanses us from all sin."

DAY 28

As you read and meditate on the following scriptures please pray for:

A growing realization and manifestation of unity in the purpose and motive of heart among Christians in the community; (PURPOSE: To bring Him pleasure, MOTIVE: For His great name's sake.)

Psalm 133:1 "Behold, how good and how pleasant it is for brethren to dwell together in unity!"

Romans 12:1-2 "I beseech *(plead)* you therefore, brethren, by the mercies of God, that you present your bodies a living sacrifice, holy, acceptable to God, which is your reasonable service. (2)And do not be conformed to this world, but be transformed by the renewing of your mind, that you may prove what is that good and acceptable and perfect will of God."

Colossians 1:17-20(a) "And He is before all things, and in Him all things consist. (18)And He is the head of the body, the Church, who is the beginning, the firstborn from the dead, that in all things He may have the preeminence. (19)For it pleased the Father that in Him all the fullness should dwell, (20)and by Him to reconcile all things..."

2 Timothy 2:19-21 "Nevertheless the solid foundation of God stands, having this seal: 'The Lord knows those who are His,' and 'Let everyone who names the name of Christ depart from iniquity.' (20)But in a great house there are not only vessels of gold and silver, but also of wood and clay, some for honor and some for dishonor. (21)Therefore if anyone cleanses himself from the latter, he will be a vessel for honor, sanctified and useful for the Master, prepared for every good work."

Other scriptures from your own study: _____

_____

A CRAFTED PRAYER

"Almighty and just Father God, help us as a community of believers and disciples to seek Your face for the strategies to pray for and repent for.

Help us to rise up in action against the growing evils in our society and culture that displease You, and threaten to bring Your righteous judgment upon this nation, (such as legalized abortion, same sex marriage, and others).

Our Father, who is in heaven, hallowed, holy and reverenced be Your name. May Your kingdom come, may your will be done, on earth, even as it is in heaven."

"WHAT'S GOD SAYING" *during your reading and prayer time?*

Notes: _____

_____

_____

_____

_____

_____

_____

List at least <u>one</u> person you can pray these scriptures for:

_____

"ONE ANOTHER" meditation for the day:

John 15:12, 17 "This is My commandment, that you love **one another** as I have loved you." "(17)These things I command you, that you love **one another**."

61

DAY 29

As you read and meditate on the following scriptures please pray for:

An increased zeal to <u>express</u> (present), <u>extend</u> (penetrate), <u>expand</u> (permeate) and <u>establish</u> (perpetuate) the kingdom of God through the evangelization and discipleship of a lost and dying Christ-rejecting world in the power of the Holy Spirit.

Matthew 28:18-20 "And Jesus came and spoke to them, saying, 'All authority has been given to Me in heaven and on earth. (19)Go therefore and make disciples of all the nations, baptizing them in the name of the Father and of the Son and of the Holy Spirit, (20)teaching them to observe all things that I have commanded you; and lo, I am with you always, even to the end of the age.' Amen."

Acts 1:8 "But you shall receive power when the Holy Spirit has come upon you; and you shall be witnesses to Me in Jerusalem, and in all Judea and Samaria, and to the end of the earth."

Colossians 1:13-14 "He *(the Father)* has delivered us *(transferred us)* from the power *(kingdom/dominion)* of darkness and conveyed us into the kingdom of the Son of His love, (14)in whom we have redemption through His blood, the forgiveness of sins."

2 Timothy 2:1-2 "You therefore, my son, be strong in the grace that is in Christ Jesus. And the things that You have heard from me among many witnesses, commit these to faithful men who will be able to teach others also."

Other scriptures from your own study: _____

_____

_____

A CRAFTED PRAYER

"Awaken Your world-wide Church to Your Spirit and display Your super-natural power in these last days, demonstrating Your victory and mastery over all the powers of darkness and works of the devil."

"WHAT'S GOD SAYING" *during your reading and prayer time?*

Notes: _____

_____

_____

_____

_____

_____

_____

_____

_____

_____

_____

List at least <u>one</u> person you can pray these scriptures for:

_____

"ONE ANOTHER" meditation for the day:

Mark 9:49-50 "For everyone will be seasoned with fire, and every sacrifice will be seasoned with salt. (50)Salt is good, but if the salt loses its flavor, how will you season it? Have salt in yourselves, and have peace with **one another**."

DAY 30

As you read and meditate on the following scriptures please pray for:

A passion for social justice based upon the Word of God.

Psalm 139:19-22 "Oh, that You would slay the wicked, O God! Depart from me, therefore, you bloodthirsty men. [20]For they speak against You wickedly; Your enemies take Your name in vain. [21]Do I not hate them, O LORD, who hate You? And do I not loathe those who rise up against You? [22]I hate them with a perfect hatred; I count them my enemies."

Psalm 145:5-9 "I will meditate on the glorious splendor of Your majesty, and on Your wondrous works. [6]Men shall speak of the might of Your awesome acts, and I will declare Your greatness. [7]They shall utter the memory of Your great goodness, and shall sing of Your righteousness. [8]The Lord is gracious and full of compassion, slow to anger and great in mercy. [9]The Lord is good to all, and His tender mercies are over all His works."

Galatians 6:7-10 "Do not be deceived, God is not mocked; for whatever a man sows, that he will also reap. [8]For he who sows to his flesh will of the flesh reap corruption, but he who sows to the Spirit will of the Spirit reap everlasting life. [9]And let us not grow weary while doing good, for in due season we shall reap if we do not lose heart. [10]Therefore, as we have opportunity, let us do good to all, especially to those who are of the household of faith."

Other scriptures from your own study: _____

_____

_____

_____

A CRAFTED PRAYER

"Rally forth an army under Your banner, King Jesus, who passionately love You and fearlessly intercede and stand up for the righteous laws and holy ways of Your kingdom throughout the entire earth, even as in heaven.

Gird our loins for action and reveal Your battle strategies to us clearly that we might hear and obey what the Spirit is saying, and join in what You are doing in the earth today. Oh, that we would rally around Your desires."

"WHAT'S GOD SAYING" *during your reading and prayer time?*

Notes: _____

_____

_____

_____

_____

_____

_____

_____

List at least <u>one</u> person you can pray these scriptures for:

_____

"**ONE ANOTHER**" meditation for the day:

1 Thessalonians 5:15 "Make sure that nobody pays back wrong for wrong, but always try to be kind to **each other** and to everyone else."   *(New International Version)*

JOURNAL

Please write down additional scriptures and personal thoughts for each of the 10 items mentioned throughout the **"30 DAY PASSAGEWAY TO REVIVAL"** *that you might have gleaned from your personal study and meditation.*

Notes: _____

_____

_____

_____

_____

_____

_____

_____

_____

_____

_____

_____

_____

_____

_____

_____

_____

_____

_____

_____

ITEM 1

An intensified awareness of God's manifest (near) presence in my daily life.

Notes: _____

_____

_____

_____

_____

_____

ITEM 2

An acute sensitivity towards sin, (a pre-emptive, preventive sensitivity), in your own life and in the life of the community... a Holy Spirit revelation and redefinition of what constitutes 'sin.'

Notes: _____

_____

_____

_____

_____

_____

_____

ITEM 3

A jealous concern for the truth of God's written word in the Bible; and the display, declaration and demonstration of the gospel of the kingdom of God in an accurate, adequate and appropriate manner in every arena of our society and culture.

Notes: _____

_____

_____

_____

_____

ITEM 4

An eagerness to hear and read the word of God as written in the Bible, and to hear and speak about the works of the Holy Spirit and our Lord... and a desperate, determined desire for and dependence upon the word of God.

Notes: _____

_____

_____

_____

_____

_____

_____

ITEM 5

An absorbing concern, concentration and commitment to intercessory prayer, praise, worship and fasting.

Notes: _____

_____

_____

_____

_____

_____

ITEM 6

An enhanced standard of conduct and holiness in my own life and in the Church throughout the community.

Notes: _____

_____

_____

_____

_____

_____

_____

_____

ITEM 7

A strengthening discernment of, concern for and loyalty towards the blood-bought Church of our Lord Jesus Christ among all its members.

Notes: _____

_____

_____

_____

_____

_____

_____

ITEM 8

A growing realization and manifestation of unity in the purpose and motive of heart among Christians in the community; (PURPOSE: To bring Him pleasure, MOTIVE: For His great name's sake.)

Notes: _____

_____

_____

_____

_____

_____

_____

ITEM 9

An increased zeal to <u>express</u> (present), <u>extend</u> (penetrate), <u>expand</u> (permeate) and <u>establish</u> (perpetuate) the kingdom of God through the evangelization and discipleship of a lost and dying Christ-rejecting world in the power of the Holy Spirit.

Notes: _____

_____

_____

_____

_____

_____

ITEM 10

A passion for social justice based upon the Word of God.

Notes: _____

_____

_____

_____

_____

_____

30 Day Passageway to Revival

Notes: _____

_____

_____

_____

_____

_____

_____

_____

_____

_____

_____

_____

_____

_____

_____

_____

_____

_____

_____

_____

_____

_____

_____

_____

_____

_____

_____

Why Fast...

When the Lord has provided so bountifully?

THE IMPORTANCE OF FASTING

The practice of fasting is an important aspect and part of a 'normal' Christian prayer life and should be a regular practice and experience of every believer and disciple of Jesus Christ.

Fasting was the practice and teaching of our Lord:

Matthew 4:1-2 "Then Jesus was led up by the Spirit into the wilderness to be tempted by the devil. (2)And when He had fasted forty days and forty nights, afterward He was hungry." *(See also Luke. 4: 1-2)*

Matthew 6:17-18 "But you, when you fast, anoint your head and wash your face, (18)so that you do not appear to men to be fasting, but to your Father who is in the secret place; and your Father who sees in secret will reward you openly.

Matthew 17:14-21 *(especially verse 21)* "However, this kind does not go out except by prayer and fasting."

Jesus said, "A disciple is not above his teacher, nor a servant above his master. It is enough for a disciple that he be like his teacher and a servant like his master." (Matthew 10:24-25(a)) This should persuade us that fasting is intended to be a part of our 'normal' Christian discipleship lifestyle.

Fasting was the practice of the early Church,

Acts 13:2-3 "As they ministered to the Lord and <u>fasted</u>, the Holy Spirit said, 'Now separate to Me Barnabas and Saul for the work to which I have called them.' (3)Then, having <u>fasted</u> and prayed, and laid hands on them, they sent them away."

For those who still look to the first century body of believers as a pattern for church life, then fasting should be included.

Other scriptures from your own study: _____

_____

_____

74

It was the practice of God's servants throughout history:

Moses:

Exodus 34:28 "So he was there with the LORD forty days and forty nights; he neither ate bread nor drank water. And He *(the LORD)* wrote on the tablets the words of the covenant, the Ten Commandments."

Samuel:

1 Samuel 7:6 "So they gathered together at Mizpah, drew water, and poured it out before the LORD. And they fasted that day, and said there, 'We have sinned against the LORD.' And Samuel judged the children of Israel at Mizpah."

David:

Psalm 35:13 "But as for me, when they were sick, my clothing was sackcloth; I humbled myself with fasting; and my prayer would return to my own heart."

2 Samuel 3:35 "And when all the people came to persuade David to eat food while it was still day, David took an oath, saying, 'God do so to me, and more also, if I taste bread or anything else till the sun goes down."

2 Samuel 12:16 "David therefore pleaded with God for the child, and David fasted and went in and lay all night on the ground."

Elijah:

1 Kings 19:8 "So he arose, and ate and drank; and he went in the strength of that food forty days and forty nights as far as Horeb, the mountain of God."

Daniel:

Daniel 9:3 "Then I set my face toward the Lord God to make request by prayer and supplication, with fasting, sackcloth and ashes."

Daniel 10:2-3 "In those days I, Daniel, was mourning three full weeks. (3)I ate no pleasant food; no meat or wine came into my mouth, nor did I anoint myself at all, till three whole weeks were fulfilled."

Ezra:

Ezra 8:23 "So we fasted and entreated our God for this, and He answered our prayers."

Ezra 10:1-8 *(especially verse 6)* "Then Ezra rose up from before the house of God, and went into the chamber of Jehohanan the son of Eliashib; and when he came there, he ate no bread and drank no water, for he mourned because of the guilt of those from the captivity."

Nehemiah:

Nehemiah 1:4 "So it was, when I heard these words, that I sat down and wept, and mourned for many days; I was fasting and praying before the God of heaven."

Paul:

Acts 9:9 "And he was three days without sight, and neither ate nor drank;"

2 Corinthians 6:5 "...in stripes, in imprisonments, in tumults, in labors, in sleeplessness, in fastings..."

2 Corinthians 11:27-28 "...in weariness, and toil, in sleeplessness often, in hunger and thirst, in fastings often, in cold and nakedness – (28)besides the other things, what comes upon me daily: my deep concern for all the churches."

There are many examples of fasting throughout both the Old and the New Testaments of the Bible, from which to establish patterns for our personal and corporate practice and application.

Notes: _____

_____

_____

_____

_____

_____

SOME OF THE VALUES OF FASTING

1. Fasting often results in deepening our spiritual brokenness and humbleness before God and men:

Deuteronomy 8:3 "So He humbled you, allowed you to hunger, and fed you with manna which you did not know nor did your fathers know, that He might make you know that man shall not live by bread alone; but man lives by every word that proceeds from the mouth of the LORD."

Psalm 35:13 "But as for me, when they were sick, my clothing was sackcloth; I humbled myself with fasting; and my prayer would return to my own heart."

Psalm 109:24-25 "My knees are weak through fasting, and my flesh is feeble from lack of fatness, (25)I have also become a reproach to them; when they look at me they shake their heads."

Daniel 10:12 "Then he said to me, 'Do not fear, Daniel, for from the first day that you set your heart to understand, and to humble yourself before your God *(with fasting)*, your words were heard; and I have come because of your words.'"

Notes: _____

_____

_____

2. Fasting may strengthen our self-control and aid in developing personal holiness and wisdom:

Daniel 1:8, 11-14, 20 "But Daniel purposed in his heart that he would not defile himself with the portion of the king's delicacies, nor with the wine which he drank; therefore he requested of the chief of the eunuchs that he might not defile himself." (11)"So Daniel said to the steward whom the chief of the eunuchs had set over Daniel, Hananiah, Mishael, and Azariah, (12)'Please test your servants for ten days, and let them give us vegetables to eat and water to drink. (13)Then let our appearance be

77

examined before you, and the appearance of the young men who eat the portion of the king's delicacies; and as you see fit, so deal with your servants.' [14]So he consented with them in this matter, and tested them ten days." [20]"And in all matters of wisdom and understanding about which the king examined them, he found them ten times better than all the magicians and astrologers who were in his realm."

Notes: _____

_____

_____

3. Fasting aids in establishing the priorities of our hearts:

Joel 2:12-13 "Now therefore,' says the LORD, 'Turn to Me with all your heart, with fasting, with weeping, and with mourning.' [13]So rend your heart, and not *(only)* your garments; return to the LORD your God, for He is gracious and merciful, slow to anger and of great kindness; and He relents from doing harm."

Matthew 4:4 "But he answered and said, 'It is written, "Man shall not live by bread alone, but by every word that proceeds from the mouth of God."' (Deuteronomy 8:3)

Notes: _____

_____

_____

4. Fasting may increase our spiritual receptivity for guidance from the Holy Spirit:

Daniel 9:3-4, 20-22 "Then I set my face toward the Lord God to make request by prayer and supplication, with fasting, sackcloth and ashes. [4]And I prayed to the Lord my God and made confession, and said 'O Lord, great and awesome God, who keeps His covenant and mercy with those who love Him, and with those who keep His commandments." "[20]Now while I was speaking, praying and confessing my sin and the sin of my people Israel, and presenting my supplication before the LORD my God for the holy mountain of my God, [21]yes, while I was speaking in prayer, the man Gabriel, whom I had seen in the vision at the beginning, being caused to fly swiftly, reached me about the time of the evening offering. [22]And he informed me, and talked with me, and said, 'O Daniel, I have now come forth to give you skill to understand.' "

Acts 10:30-31 "So Cornelius said, 'Four days ago I was fasting until this hour; and at the ninth hour I prayed in my house, and behold, a man stood before me in bright clothing, [31]and said, 'Cornelius, your prayer has been heard, and your alms are remembered in the sight of God. [32] Send therefore to Joppa and call Simon here, whose surname is Peter. He is lodging in the house of Simon, a tanner, by the sea. When he comes, he will speak to you.'

Acts 13:2 "As they ministered to the Lord and fasted, the Holy Spirit said, 'Now separate to Me Barnabas and Saul for the work to which I have called them.' "

Acts 14:23 "So when they had appointed elders in every church, and prayed with fasting, they commended them to the Lord in whom they had believed."

Acts 27:21-25 "But after long abstinence from food, then Paul stood in the midst of them and said, 'Men, you should have listened to me, and not have sailed from Crete and incurred this disaster and loss. [22]And now I urge you to take heart, for there will be no loss of life among you, but only the ship. [23]For there stood by me this night an angel of the God to whom I belong and whom I serve, [24] saying, 'Do not be afraid, Paul; you must be brought before Caesar; and indeed God has granted you all those who sail with you.' [25]Therefore, take heart, men, for I believe God that it will be just as it was told to me.' "

Notes: _____

_____

5. Fasting will often strengthen the exercise of our spiritual authority:

Matthew 17:18-19, 21 "And Jesus rebuked the demon, and he came out of him; and the child was cured from that very hour. (19)The disciples came to Jesus privately and said, 'Why could we not cast him out?' (21)'However, this kind does not go out except by prayer and fasting.' "

Luke 4:1-2 "Then Jesus, being filled with the Holy Spirit, returned from the Jordan and was led by the Spirit into the wilderness, (2)being tempted for forty days by the devil. And in those days He ate nothing, and afterward, when they had ended, He was hungry."

Luke 4:14 "Then Jesus returned in the power of the Spirit to Galilee, and news of Him went out through all the surrounding region."

Notes: _____

_____

6. Fasting may result in breaking the enemy's hold on the hearts and souls of men:

Isaiah 58:6 "Is this not the fast that I have chosen: to loose the bonds of wickedness, to undo the heavy burdens, to let the oppressed go free, and that you break every yoke?"

Matthew 17:21 "However, this kind does not go out except by prayer and fasting."

Notes: _____

_____

_____

7. Fasting will often serve to intensify our personal and corporate prayer efforts:

2 Chronicles 20:3-4 "And Jehoshaphat feared, and set himself to seek the LORD, and proclaimed a fast throughout all Judah. (4)So Judah gathered together to ask help from the Lord; and from all the cities of Judah they came to seek the LORD."

Ezra 8:21-23 "Then I proclaimed a fast there at the river of Ahava, that we might humble ourselves before our God, to seek from Him the right way for us and our little ones and all our possessions. (22)For I was ashamed to request of the king an escort of soldiers and horsemen to help us against the enemy on the road, because we had spoken to the king, saying 'The hand of God is upon all those for good who seek Him, but His power and His wrath are against all those who forsake Him.' (23)So we fasted and entreated our God for this, and He answered our prayer."

Joel 1:13-15 "Gird yourselves and lament, you priests; wail, you who minister before the altar; come, lie all night in sackcloth, you who minister to my God; for the grain offering and drink offering are withheld from the house of your God. (14)Consecrate a fast, call a sacred assembly; gather the elders and all the inhabitants of the land into the house of the Lord your God, and cry out to the Lord. (15)Alas for the day! For the day of the Lord is at hand; it shall come as destruction from the Almighty."

8: Fasting is a legitimate ministry unto the Lord:

Luke 2:36-37 "Now there was one, Anna, a prophetess, the daughter of Phanuel, of the tribe of Asher. She was of a great age, and had lived with a husband seven years from her virginity; (37)and this woman was a widow of about eighty-four years, who did not depart from the temple, but served God with fastings and prayers night and day."

Notes: _____

_____

_____

9. Fasting will enlarge our spiritual usefulness to the kingdom of God by accomplishing everything mentioned in points 1 through 8 in your life.

VARIOUS LENGTHS OF FASTING

The Bible records several different lengths or periods of fasting:

1. All day:

Judges 20:26 "Then all the children of Israel, that is, all the people, went up and came to the house of God and wept. They sat there before the LORD and fasted that day until evening; and they offered burnt offerings and peace offerings before the LORD."

1 Samuel 7:6 "So they gathered together at Mizpah, drew water, and poured it out before the LORD. And they fasted that day, and said there, 'We have sinned against the LORD.' And Samuel judged the children of Israel at Mizpah."

Ezra 9:3-5 "So when I heard this thing, I tore my garment and my robe, and plucked out some of the hair of my head and beard, and sat down astonished. (4)Then everyone who trembled at the words of the God of Israel assembled to me, because of the transgression of those who had been carried away captive, and I sat astonished until the evening sacrifice. (5)At the evening sacrifice I arose from my fasting; and having torn my garment and my robe, I fell on my knees and spread out my hands to the LORD my God."

Jeremiah 36:6 "You go, therefore, and read from the scroll which you have written at my instruction, the words of the LORD in the hearing of the people in the LORD'S house on the day of fasting. And you shall also read them in the hearing of all of Judah who come from their cities."

Notes: _____

_____

_____

_____

_____

2. All night:

Daniel 6:18 "Now the king went to his palace and spent the night fasting; and no musicians were brought before him. Also his sleep went from him."

Notes: _____

_____

_____

3. Three days:

Acts 9:9 "And he was three days without sight, and neither ate nor drank."

Notes: _____

_____

_____

4. Seven days:

1 Samuel 31:13 "Then they took their bones and buried them under the tamarisk tree at Jabesh, and fasted seven days."

2 Samuel 12:16-18 "David therefore pleaded with God for the child, and David fasted and went in and lay all night on the ground. (17)So the elders of his house arose and went to him, to raise him up from the ground. But he would not, nor did he eat food with them. (18) Then on the seventh day it came to pass that the child died..."

Notes: _____

_____

_____

_____

_____

5. Ten days:

Daniel 1:11-14 "So Daniel said to the steward whom the chief of the eunuchs had set over Daniel, Hananiah, Mishael, and Azariah, (12)'Please test your servants for ten days, and let them give us vegetables to eat and water to drink. (13)Then let our appearance be examined before you, and the appearance of the young men who eat the portion of the king's delicacies; and as you see fit, so deal with your servants. (14)So he consented with them in this matter, and tested them ten days."

Notes: _____

_____

6. Three weeks

Daniel 10:2-3 "In those days I, Daniel, was mourning three full weeks. (3)I ate no pleasant food; no meat or wine came into my mouth, nor did I anoint myself at all, till three whole weeks were fulfilled."

Notes: _____

_____

7. Forty days:

1 Kings 19:8 "So he arose, and ate and drank; and he went in the strength of that food forty days and forty nights as far as Horeb, the mountain of God."
(See also Moses in Exodus 34:28, and Jesus in Matthew 4:1-2)

For some believers, missing a single meal is a *'true sacrifice'* and that may be where to begin. Then, as the Holy Spirit leads, you will be able to extend the length and intensity of fasting in your life, and perhaps the various types of fasting as well.

Notes: _____

_____

_____

LOSS OF BENEFITS - THE MOTIVE FOR FASTING

We will lose any and all the benefits or value of fasting if:

1. We are trying to manipulate God:

Isaiah 58:3 "'Why have we fasted,' they say, 'and You have not seen? Why have we afflicted our souls, and You take no notice?' In fact, in the day of your fast you find pleasure, and exploit all your laborers."

2. We do it to impress others:

Matthew 6:16-18 "Moreover, when you fast, do not be like the hypocrites, with a sad countenance. For they disfigure their faces that they may appear to men to be fasting. Assuredly, I say to you, they have their reward. (17)But you, when you fast, anoint your head and wash your face, (18)so that you do not appear to men to be fasting, but to your Father who is in the secret place; and your Father who sees in secret will reward you openly."

Luke 18:11-12 "The Pharisee stood and prayed thus with himself, 'God, I thank You that I am not like other men; extortionist, unjust, adulterers, or even as this tax collector. (12)I fast twice a week; I give tithes of all that I possess.' I tell you... everyone who exalts himself will be humbled, and he who humbles himself will be exalted."

3. We allow it to be an excuse for not being 'civil':

Isaiah 58:4 "Indeed you fast for strife and debate, and to strike with the fist of wickedness. You will not fast as you do this day, to make your voice heard on high."

Notes: _____

_____

_____

_____

_____

HOW TO FAST

Your times of prayer and fasting should be done:

1. With an honest searching heart:

Zechariah 7:4-7 "Then the word of the Lord of hosts came to me, saying, (5)'Say to all the people of the land, and to the priests: "When you fasted and mourned in the fifth and seventh months during those seventy years, did you really fast for Me – for Me? (6)When you eat and when you drink, do you not eat and drink for yourselves? (7)Should you not have obeyed the words which the Lord proclaimed through the former prophets when Jerusalem and the cities around it were inhabited and prosperous, and the South and the Lowland were inhabited?"

2. With weeping and true repentance:

Joel 2:12 "Now therefore," says the Lord, "turn to Me with all your heart, with fasting, with weeping, and with mourning."

3. It can be done privately:

Matthew 6:6 "But you, when you pray, go into your room, and when you have shut your door, pray to your Father who is in the secret place; and your Father who sees in secret will reward you openly."

4. It can be done with others with a common motive:

Nehemiah. 9:1-3 "Now on the twenty-fourth day of this month the children of Israel were assembled with fasting, in sackcloth and with dust on their heads. (2)Then those of Israelite lineage separated themselves from all foreigners; and they stood and confessed their sins and the iniquities of their fathers. (3)And they stood up in their place and read from the Book of the Law of the LORD their God for one-fourth of the day; and for another fourth they confessed and worshiped the LORD their God."

If you have never fasted before, go slowly at first, but do go. You might want to start with a partial 'Daniel' fast.

Daniel 1:12 "Please test your servants for ten days, and let them give us vegetables to eat and water to drink."

As you mature in the practice of fasting, the Holy Spirit may, at times, lead you into an 'absolute' fast for 1-2 days. Total fasts longer than this are a health concern, and should be undertaken with caution and supervision/assistance.

Esther 4:16 "Go, gather all the Jews who are present in Shushan, and fast for me; neither eat nor drink for three days night or day. My maids and I will fast likewise. And so I will go to the king, which is against the law; and if I perish, I perish!"

Nehemiah 1:4 "So it was, when I heard these words that I sat down and wept, and mourned for many days: I was fasting and praying before the God of heaven."

At all times remember that it is the *'posture'* of our heart which God witnesses and approves, not simply the *'lack of food on our plate.'*

Other scriptures from your own study: _____

_____

_____

_____

_____

_____

_____

_____

_____

_____

_____

_____

PRACTICAL TIPS FOR FASTING

1. The early Church gave themselves to fasting and prayer for a time. If they needed it then, we need it now! Every time you pray and fast for a certain amount of time, you are investing in a powerful kingdom – the kingdom of God.

Notes: _____

_____

_____

2. Set a definite time for your fast so you know in advance how long you will be fasting. Keep in mind that fasting changes your heart. A one-day, or one-meal fast can be very powerful when submitted to God as a sacrifice of your appetites, self-determination, or sense of 'entitlement' before the Lord.

Notes: _____

_____

_____

3. Since you are denying your flesh and seeking the Lord, you may find yourself in the midst of spiritual warfare and thus becoming irritable, or even unable or unwilling to pray. Some of these feelings may be induced just because of a physical reaction; plan beforehand to 'pray through' the spiritual confrontations and battle.

Notes: _____

_____

_____

4. Try to rest if you feel weak, and get some fresh air every day. A brief walk and mild exercise is beneficial during a fast.

Notes: _____

_____

_____

5. Spend time reading scripture, worshiping, and praying. Use the time you would normally spend eating or preparing food for 'spiritual exercise.' Many people have noticed that the Bible simply comes alive while they are fasting.

Notes: _____

_____

_____

6. Have specific spiritual goals that you desire to obtain while praying and fasting. Without prayer and a set purpose, fasting is only a glorified diet.

Notes: _____

_____

_____

7. If your fast has been for several days it is good to beak your fast with juice, fresh fruits, steamed vegetables, bread or rice, adding other foods in a day or two. Avoid meat, and fats for several meals or days depending on the length of the fast you have undertaken. Keep in mind your stomach has been inactive and it takes a while to restore essential digestive enzymes and acids. Fasting is a very natural and even healing processes for your body, so do not undo your efforts with unhealthy, 'junk' foods after your fast.

Notes: _____

_____

_____

_____

8. Some medical conditions are prohibitive to fasting. Get the advice of your physician if you have a medical condition. These conditions include diabetes, hypoglycemia, and heart disease. Pregnant and nursing mothers also should not fast because it will deprive the body of necessary nutrients. Also some medications need to be taken with food so use discretion. In these cases where you are unable to do a complete fast (water only) consider abstaining from television or conversation, and dedicating yourself to prayer during this time. Be careful of 'light-headedness' while fasting. Be prepared in advance how you will cope with such conditions.

Notes: _____

_____

_____

9. Other types of fasts may include:

'Three day water, honey and lemon' - This is considered a 'cleansing fast.' Squeeze ½ a lemon in a cup of hot water and add honey to taste. Drink water throughout the day. This can be used for an extended fast.

'Juice only fast' (or fast with only fruits or vegetables and water) - This is a good fast for those who have physically demanding jobs.

Notes: _____

_____

_____

_____

_____

_____

_____

OTHER FORMS OF FASTING

Do not limit fasting to only the abstinence of food. Allow the Holy Spirit to lead you in other expressions of fasting. For example, you may also want to consider "seasons" of fasting from: the media (television, radio, newspapers, magazines, etc.), people (complete isolation unto the Lord Himself, a single person retreat, etc.), conversation (speak to no one except the Lord for just one day and it will change your life), and sex (as mentioned in *I Corinthians 7:5*).

1 Corinthians 7:5 "Do not deprive one another except with consent for a time, that you may give yourselves to fasting and prayer; and come together again so that Satan does not tempt you because of your lack of self-control."

Allow the Lord to show you what type, length and fashion of fast would be pleasing and acceptable to Him to accomplish His purposes and intents. Allow the Holy Spirit to guide your fast; the beginning, the manner, the purpose... everything.

Fasting, in whatever form it might be practiced, is simply the practice of self-denial, not for our sake, but for His great name's sake. Take just a moment to consider the words of our Lord in *Luke 9:23* and then decide what to do.

Luke 9:23 "Then He said to them all, 'If anyone desires to come after Me, let him deny himself, and take up his cross daily, and follow Me.'"

Notes: _____

_____

_____

_____

_____

_____

_____

A FEW FASTING SCRIPTURES:

Moses	Exodus 34:28
Samuel	1 Samuel 7:6
Israelites	Judges 20:26
Daniel	Daniel 9:3, 10:2-3
David	2 Samuel 3:35, 12:16; Psalm 35:13
Elijah	1 Kings 19:8
Ezra	Ezra 8:21-23, 10:1-8
Darius	Daniel 6:9, 18
Nehemiah	Nehemiah 1:4; 9:1-3
Ninevites	Jonah 3:5-10
Jehoshaphat	(2 Chronicles 20:1-3)
Jesus	Matthew 4:1-2, 6:17-18, 17:14-21
Anna	Luke 2:36-37
John's Disciples	Mark 2:18
Christians	Acts 13:2-3
Paul	Acts 9:9; 2 Corinthians 6:5, 11:27

Other scriptures from your own study: _____

_____

_____

_____

_____

_____

_____

_____

_____

_____

_____

_____

_____

30 Day Passageway to Revival

Notes: _____

_____

_____

_____

_____

_____

_____

_____

_____

_____

_____

_____

_____

_____

_____

_____

_____

_____

_____

_____

_____

_____

_____

_____

_____

_____

_____

LIST OF 'ONE ANOTHER' SCRIPTURES:

Mark 9:49-50 "For everyone will be seasoned with fire, and every sacrifice will be seasoned with salt. (50)Salt is good, but if the salt loses its flavor, how will you season it? Have salt in yourselves, and have peace with **one another**."

John 13:14 "If I then, your Lord and Teacher, have washed your feet, you also ought to wash **one another's** feet. For I have given you an example that you should do as I have done to you."

John 13:34-35 "A new commandment I give to you, that you love **one another**; as I have loved you, that you also love **one another**. (35)By this all will know that you are My disciples, if you have love for **one another**."

John 15:12, 17 "This is My commandment, that you love **one another** as I have loved you." "(17)These things I command you, that you love **one another**."

Romans 12:3-5 "For I say, through the grace given to me, to everyone who is among you, not to think of himself more highly than he ought to think, but to think soberly, as God has dealt to each one a measure of faith. (4)For as we have many members in one body, but all the members do not have the same function, (5)so we being many, are one body in Christ, and individually members of **one another**."

Romans 12:9-13 "Let love be without hypocrisy. Abhor what is evil. Cling to what is good. (10)Be kindly affectionate to **one another** with brotherly love, in honor giving preference to **one another**; (11)not lagging in diligence, fervent in spirit, serving the Lord; (12)rejoicing in hope, patient in tribulation, continuing steadfast in prayer; (13)distributing to the needs of the saints, given to hospitality."

Romans 12:15-16 "Rejoice with those who rejoice, and weep with those who weep. (16)Be of the same mind toward **one**

another. Do not set your mind on high things, but associate with the humble. Do not be wise in your own opinion."

Romans 13:8 "Owe no man anything except to love **one another**, for he who loves another has fulfilled the Law."

Romans 14:13 "Therefore let us not judge **one another** anymore, but rather resolve this, not to put a stumbling block or a cause to fall in our brother's way."

Romans 15:5-7 "Now may the God of patience and comfort grant you to be like-minded toward **one another**, according to Christ Jesus, (6)that you may with one mind and one mouth glorify the God and Father of our Lord Jesus Christ. (7)Therefore receive **one another**, just as Christ also received us, to the glory of God."

Romans 15:14 "Now I myself am confident concerning you, my brethren, that you also are full of goodness, filled with all knowledge, able also to admonish **one another**."

Romans 16:16 "Greet **one another** with a holy kiss. The churches of Christ greet you."

1 Corinthians 11:27-29, 33 "Therefore whoever eats this bread or drinks this cup of the Lord in an unworthy manner will be guilty of the body and the blood of the Lord. (28)But let a man examine himself, and so let him eat of the bread and drink of the cup. (29)For he who eats and drinks in an unworthy manner eats and drinks judgment to himself, not discerning the Lord's body. (33)Therefore, my brethren, when you come together to eat, wait for **one another**."

1 Corinthians 12:24(b)-27 "...but God composed the body, having given greater honor to that part which lacks it, (25)that there should be no schism in the body; but that the members should have the same care for **one another**. (26)And if one member suffers, all the members suffer with it; or if one member is honored, all the members rejoice with it. (27)Now you are the body of Christ, and members individually."

Galatians 5:13-14 "For you, brethren, have been called in liberty; only do not use liberty as an opportunity for the flesh, but through love serve **one another**. (14)For all of the law is fulfilled in one word, even in this: '*You shall love your neighbor as yourself.*' "   *(Leviticus 19:18)*

Galatians 6:1-2 "Brethren, if a man is overtaken in any trespass, you who are spiritual restore such a one in a spirit of gentleness, considering yourself lest you also be tempted. (2)Bear **one another's** burdens, and so fulfill the law of Christ."

Ephesians 4:31-32 "Let all bitterness, wrath, anger, clamor and evil speaking be put away from you, with all malice. (32)And be kind to **one another**, tenderhearted, forgiving **one another**, even as God in Christ forgave you."

Ephesians 5:18-21 "And do not be drunk with wine, in which is dissipation; but be filled with the Spirit, (19)speaking to **one another** in psalms and hymns and spiritual songs, singing and making melody in your heart to the Lord, (20)giving thanks always for all things to God the Father, in the name of our Lord Jesus Christ, (21)submitting to **one another** in the fear of God."

Colossians 3:12-13 "Therefore, as the elect of God, holy and beloved, put on tender mercies, kindness, humility, meekness, longsuffering; **(13)**bearing with **one another**, and forgiving **one another**, if anyone has a complaint against another; even as Christ forgave you, so you also must do."

Colossians 3:14-17 "But above all these things put on love, which is the bond of perfection. (15)And let the peace of God rule in your hearts, to which also you were called in one body; and be thankful. (16)Let the word of Christ dwell in you richly in all wisdom, teaching and admonishing **one another** is psalms and hymns and spiritual songs, singing with grace in your hearts to the Lord."

1 Thessalonians 3:12-13 "And may the Lord make you increase and abound in love to **one another** and to all, just as we do to you, (13)so that He may establish your hearts blameless in holiness before our God and Father at the coming of our Lord Jesus Christ with all His saints."

1 Thessalonians 4:16-18 "For the Lord Himself will descend from heaven with a shout, with the voice of an archangel, and with the trumpet of God. And the dead in Christ will rise first. (17)Then we who are alive and remain shall be caught up together with them in the clouds to meet the Lord in the air. And thus we shall always be with the Lord. (18)Therefore comfort **one another** with these words."

1 Thessalonians 5:9-11 "For God did not appoint us to wrath, but to obtain salvation through our Lord Jesus Christ, (10)who died for us, that whether we wake or sleep, we should live together with Him. (11)Therefore comfort **each other** and edify **one another**, just as you are also doing."

1 Thessalonians 5:15 "Make sure that nobody pays back wrong for wrong, but always try to be kind to **each other** and to everyone else." (NIV)

Hebrews 10:23-25 "Let us hold fast the confession of our faith, for He who promised is faithful. (24)And let us consider **one another** in order to stir up love and good works, (25)not forsaking the assembling of ourselves together, as is the manner of some, but exhorting **one another**, and so much the more as you see the Day approaching."

James 4:11-12 "Do not speak evil of **one another**, brethren. He who speaks evil of a brother and judges his brother, speaks evil of the law and judges the law. But if you judge the law, you are not a doer of the law but a judge. (12)There is one Lawgiver, who is able to save and destroy. Who are you to judge **another**?"

James 5:16 "Confess your trespasses *(faults, sins)* to **one another**, and pray for **one another**, that you may be healed. The effective, fervent prayer of a righteous man *(on behalf of another)* avails much."

1 Peter 4:7-10 "But the end of all things is at hand, therefore be serious and watchful in your prayers. (8)And above all things have fervent love for **one another**, for 'love will cover a multitude of sins.' (9)Be hospitable to **one another**, without grumbling. (10)As each one has received a gift, minister it to **one another**, as good stewards of the manifold grace of God."

1 Peter 5:5-7 "Likewise you younger people, submit yourselves to your elders. Yes, all of you be submissive to **one another**, and be clothed in humility, for 'God resists the proud, but gives grace to the humble.' (6)Therefore humble yourselves under the mighty hand of God, that He may exalt you in due time, (7)casting all your cares upon Him, for He cares for you."

1 John 1:5-7 "This is the message which we have heard from Him and declare to you, that God is light and in Him is no darkness at all. (6)If we say that we have fellowship with Him, and walk in darkness, we lie and do not practice the truth. (7)But if we walk in the light as He is in the light, we have fellowship with **one another**. And the blood of Jesus Christ His Son cleanses us from all sin."

1 John 3:10-11 "In this the children of God and the children of the devil are manifest: whoever does not practice righteousness is not of God, nor is he who does not love his brother. (11)For this is the message that you heard from the beginning, that we should love **one another**..."

1 John 3:22-23 "And whatever we ask we receive from Him, because we keep His commandments and do those things that are pleasing in His sight. (23)And this is His commandment: that we should believe on the name of His

Son Jesus Christ and love **one another**, as He gave us commandment."

1 John 4:7-8 "Beloved, let us love **one another**, for love is of God; and everyone who loves is born of God and knows God. (8)He who does not love does not know God, for God is love."

Other scriptures from your own study: _____

_____

_____

_____

_____

_____

_____

_____

_____

_____

_____

_____

_____

_____

_____

_____

_____

_____

_____

_____

_____

_____

While reading "The Church Triumphant at The End of The Age" by Nate Krupp in 1988, I was challenged by the prospect of the promises of God's Word for revival, restoration, unity, world evangelization and persecution.

Among the wealth of historical information and current global statistics, I found two lists composed by two respected men of God of recent history: one a Methodist leader, Dr. A. Skevington Wood; and the other a Baptist leader, Charles Spurgeon. Inspired by these two lists I developed a single list of 10 points, which became a foundation for a booklet entitled, "The Pearl of Revival," published in 1989. Since then I have used this same list in many different formats.

This small book, "*30 DAY PASSAGEWAY TO REVIVAL*," is an effort to unite together in prayer as many people as possible with a focused purpose. I have come to believe that, in faithfulness to His word, the Lord shall respond to the united cry of His people with an outpouring and sovereign move of His Spirit that will historically impact our societies and cultures throughout the earth one precious soul at a time.

As you read through and meditate on each day of the calendar, I hope that you will pray for revival within your own life, your community, and for spiritual awakening among the multitudes lost without hope in Christ. This is both a privilege and a responsibility available only to us as disciples of Jesus Christ.

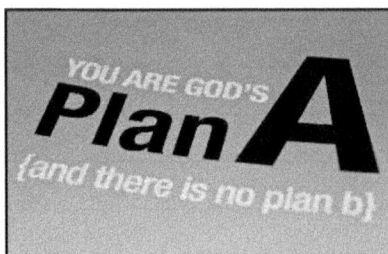

No one else on the face of the earth has such an awesome opportunity to impact the destiny of mankind in this hour as we do, as we unite our hearts together with others in fervent, concerted prayer for revival and spiritual awakening.

Thank you for responding to this 'call to arms' and taking your place as a servant of prayer.

OTHER BOOKS AVAILABLE FROM DAVID C. WOODRUM

Imitate Me as I Imitate Christ

A Reformational, Restorational, Repairing and Guarding Manual

Kingdom Exploration

Bridging Two Worlds

Notes: _____

_____

_____

_____

_____

_____

_____

_____

_____

_____

_____

_____

_____

_____

_____

_____

_____

_____

_____

_____

_____

_____

_____

_____

_____

_____

_____

Notes: _____

_____

_____

_____

_____

_____

_____

_____

_____

_____

_____

_____

_____

_____

_____

_____

_____

_____

_____

_____

_____

_____

_____

_____

30 Day Passageway to Revival

Notes: _____

_____

_____

_____

_____

_____

_____

_____

_____

_____

_____

_____

_____

_____

_____

_____

_____

_____

_____

_____

_____

_____

_____

_____

_____

_____

30 Day Passageway to Revival

Notes: _____

_____

_____

_____

_____

_____

_____

_____

_____

_____

_____

_____

_____

_____

_____

_____

_____

_____

_____

_____

_____

_____

_____

_____

_____

_____

_____

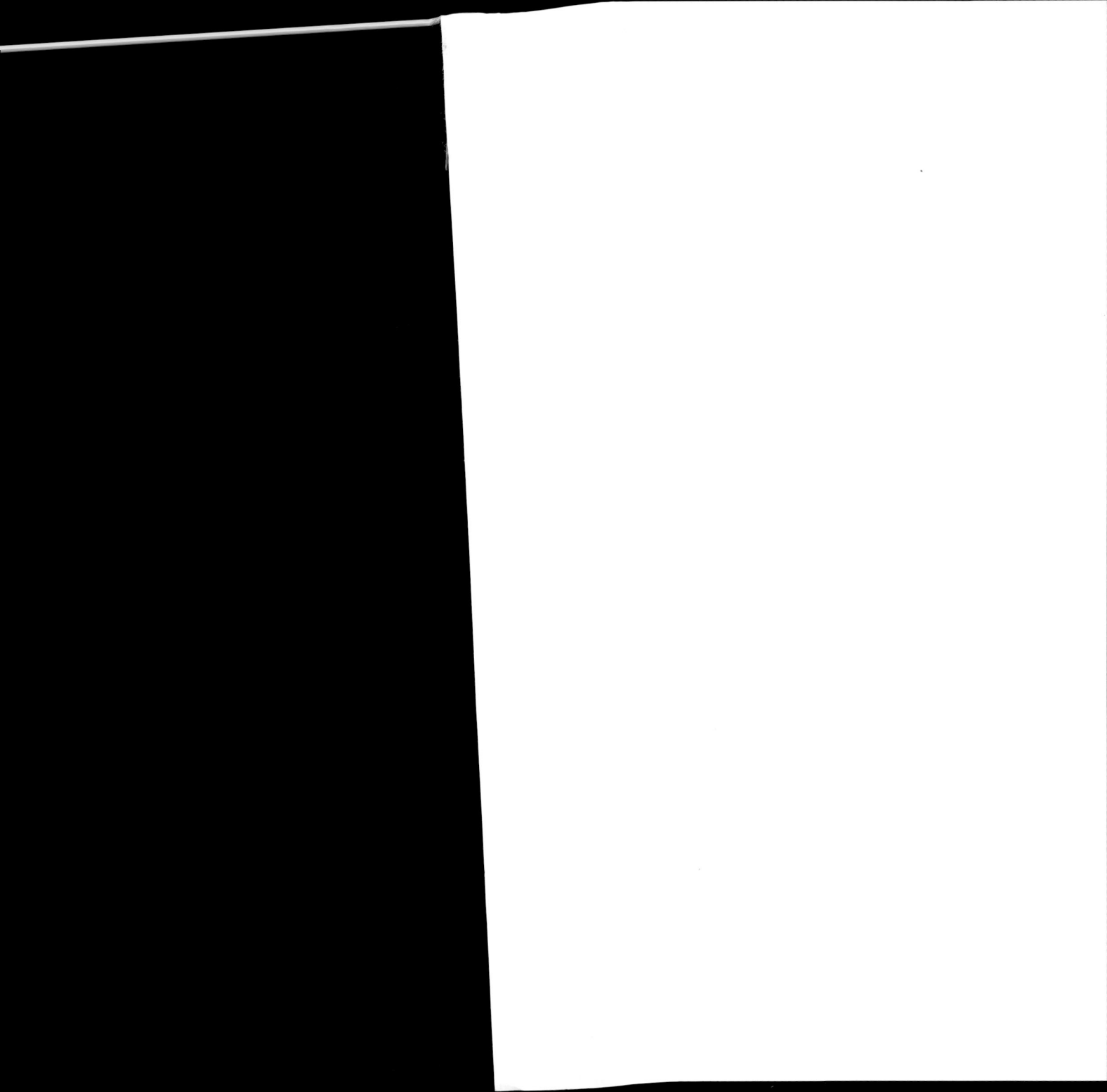